# Around the Buoys

## Bill Backshall

*Inserting the Golden Key into the Memory Locker*

SPINETINGLERS
PUBLISHING

Around the Buoys

By Bill Backshall

ISBN - 978-1-906657-38-3

Spinetinglers Publishing
22 Vestry Road
Co. Down
BT23 6HJ
UK
www.spinetinglerspublishing.com

© 2015 Bill Backshall. All rights reserved.

No part of this book may be reproduced, stored in a retrieval system, or, transmitted by any means without the written permission of the author.

This book has been formatted by
Spinetinglers Publishing
UK

Other Books,

All over the Place

Small Boat, Spun Yarn.

Swing the Liverpool Lamp

Short Change

Clinging to the Wreckage

*Bill Backshall*

From the Dockside streets of Liverpool a young man stands guard of his much loved home with Rex, his faithful companion. He dreams of later travelling the world at sea on one of the thousands of ships that once docked regularly in Liverpool.

That era has gone in the name of progress, but Bill has delved into his Sea Bag, inserted the golden key into his memory locker and revealed a brimming cap full of anecdotes of life in the Merchant Navy.

Sadly future generations will never know that way of life and we can only grieve for them. They will truly never know what they have missed. But this book will give them an insight into a world where boys became men, who

*Around the Buoys*

quickly adapted to their responsibilities, particularly throughout the ravages of two world wars.

*Bill Backshall*

## Seafarers Technical Phrases
## No1

| | |
|---|---|
| Banjo Fleet | Awkward stretch of paintwork |
| Burn Down | Decline to report. Bad discharge |
| Bell to Bell | Rigid discipline, no leeway |
| Bloods | Passengers with tipping potential |
| Brothel Creepers | Soft sandals |
| Carrying a passenger | A lazy/incompetent shipmate |
| Clinging to the wreckage | At the bitter end of things |
| Cunard Yank | Seafarer who adopts U.S styles |
| Duck muck and hailstones | Curry and rice |
| Eleven Trips in Her | One out and one home |
| Give it a Passage | To dispose of overboard |
| Got the Channels | Nearing home port excitement |
| He's swinging Your Compass | He's conning you |
| A Holiday | Missed part when painting |
| Lying in the Lee of Bum Island | Sleeping accompanied |
| More Days, More Dollars | Compensation for extended trip |
| Out of the Game | Drunk/unconscious |
| Red Lead | Tomato soup |
| Schooner Rigged | Poorly dressed /equipped |
| Swingin' the Lamp | Blowing about old seafaring day |
| Starting Gear | Knife, fork, spoon |
| Steam Queen | Liner laundress |
| Shellback | Old seafarer |
| Two Blocks | As far as it goes |
| Turned in on the Rake | Sleeping unwashed & still dressed |
| Wristwatch A B | Modern seaman with toiletries |

*Around the Buoys*

## No 2

| | |
|---|---|
| Around the Buoys | Second helping of soup, duff etc |
| Blowing for Tugs | Physically exhausted |
| Bedroom Stewards Feet | One at 10 to, one at 10 past |
| Big Forced Draught Job | Buxom Lady |
| Crab fat in the Chain Locker | Treatment for infestation |
| Dragging his Anchor | Seafarer is dying |
| Dirty Burner | Male venereal complaint |
| "I'll Trim your Vents" | Physical attack threatened |
| In Shallow Water | Precarious financial position |
| Lower the Boom | Apply financial aid pressure |
| Nobby Clark | Shark |
| Mine Sweeping | Supping unattended drinks |
| On Soundings | Alcohol bottle contents low |
| Pearl Diving | Washing dirty dishes etc |
| She's Down by the Head | Excessive illegal swag forward |
| South About | Alternative physical approach |
| Seagull Rigged | Scrawny but voracious diner |
| Twin Screw | Seaman with effeminate inclination |
| The Big Locker | Porthole (For unwanted goods) |
| Vents on the Wind | Eavesdropping |
| Wollyback | Seafarer from rural areas |

*Bill Backshall*

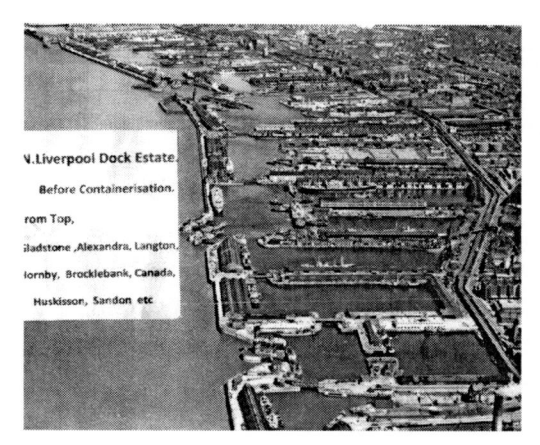

**Liverpool Docks 1940.**

**Impressions**

N.Liverpool Dock Estate.
Before Containerisation.
rom Top,
iladstone ,Alexandra, Langton,
lornby, Brocklebank, Canada,
Huskisson, Sandon etc

One of my first working days as a bewildered fourteen year old commenced aboard an Ellerman Lines "City" boat with worrisome moments crossing the gangway over the yawning chasm of the cavernous dry dock. My senses then registered the following impressions, beginning with the urgency of work people as they busily prepared the vessel for another dangerous wartime voyage.

Then came the constant head aching noise of riveters and scalers rattling and chipping away, next the strange dry dock reek of boot topping and oxide being painted on the lower hull, mixing with the stench of the river bed mud covered anchor chains being hosed clean. The sweet smell of freshly sawn redwood timber and the pungent smell of molten asphalt as it was poured into the wooden mouldings that joiners had encased the bridge and wheel house with, reinforcing them for A.A defence.

The wheel house and chartroom themselves strangely deserted, forsaken in the harbour. The continual white feather and hiss of steam from the funnel as it discharged waste water into the atmosphere. The working alleyway

*Around the Buoys*

draughting the appetising odour of soup, boiling veg and duff from the galley, changing at times to a blast of hot oily air coupled with the odd whiff of paint from hidden decorators.

The cleanliness and highly polished metalwork of the engine room from where that hot oil smelling air gushed. Lascar engine room seamen quietly but continually polishing away at hot gleaming hand rails. Most noises being overcome by the deafening bell ringing as the telegraphs' were overhauled and then repeatedly tested and retested.

The warm, relaxing, comfort of the recently vacated passenger's cabins with Canadian and Yankee magazines still lying around. The lingering sweet smell of the discharged countless apples fighting to overcome the exotic smell of raisins, sultanas etc. With spilt layers of the same sticking to the steel deck plates, then being trodden underfoot and transferred to footwear. The peculiar burning smoke of the gas welders and the blinding flashes, blue smoke, and crackling of the electric arc welders as they cut and adjusted steelwork with attendants standing close with water buckets for safety measures.

Whiffs of the unusual, but pleasing "Sweet Caporal" and "Lucky Strike" tobacco smoke as ship repairmen loitered in the fiddly for a warm and a drag of the recently crew bartered overseas 'ciggies'. The breeze, carrying the strong smell of curried meals from the Lascars' quarters aft and the luxurious appetiser of morning coffee from the main saloon.

The laughter, singing and cheerful chatter of cleaning ladies in their coarse aprons as they scrubbed decks with stiff hand brushes, soap bars and pine disinfectant water. The intoxicating ship smell of Stockholm tar spun yarn, the ropey smell of wet mooring lines from focsul' and poop and the horrible whiff of fish oil from the overhauled stays and running gear. The flapping of the masthead blue house flag with J R E in white written on it only heard when the ear shattering, clattering steam shrouded winches also under repair were thankfully silenced after being test run. Finally, the last memory that registered, the mixed smells of floating spilt fuel oil, dead fish, jetsam, salty dunnage timber, boot topping and oxide paint wind trapped in the corner of the nearby Gladstone Dock as I walked home drunk with the sights, smells and sounds of shipping, knowing I was hooked, knowing my ambition to be a seafarer was now confirmed.

**Crabby**

Coming down from the wheel, I tried to be nautical by saying to Johnny,

"The clinometer registers a near permanent 15 degree list to starboard."

"Gerraway!" He replied, looking suitably impressed, then he spoilt it all by saying,

"Not only that Bill, have you noticed she's leaning to the right all the time?"

We'd left Sweden with every plank of timber that country had produced in the last year or two, with hatches full, and the stuff stacked on deck damn near table high. In rough weather we'd soon developed a nasty list. The old shellbacks aboard told us not to worry, it was quite usual when the seas soak the weather side timber and with deals becoming loose and being lost on the lee, It upsets the trim of the dish.

So, OK, we accepted that and transferred our worries to trying to walk upright combating the continual list and thus developing what the same old timers called "Crabby." This means adjusting the right leg to extend longer and the left one to shorten up a bit, then reversing the operation when walking aft. The results made us look like we were practising the 'Hokey-Kokey' at times, but after some days at sea with every step taken aboard being adjusted it gradually becomes an automatic response.

This was all very helpful at sea, but when berthed in the Canada dock Liverpool after the passage, the legs themselves decide to persist with the regime for an hour or so and continue to make walking awkward with the body wanting to lean 15 degrees to port or starboard. The stevedores kindly accepted this, pretending not to notice, probably used to seeing other timber boat seamen similarly handicapped. Incidentally, returning aboard after alcoholic refreshment, a seafarer's body inclination is treated by them as a separate matter.

Discharging the bulk timber now meant that pieces were scattered around untidily like madman's urine and whilst throwing a deal aside out of my way, a large splinter pierced the end of my middle finger. Finding it had gone straight through and was emerging from the other side, I panicked and jumped a lift to Walton Hospital, which saw me 'Crabbying' badly into the A & E department where a Doctor after digging away, finally withdrew the damned thing.

He then recommended a tetanus injection, so lowering my trousers half-mast; he then shoved a large needle full into the top of my thigh. After a few minutes it began to pain, so that when walking to the exit I was really struggling and limping badly what with the injection and the "Crabby" effect still persisting. Spotting a visitors snack bar I decided upon a rest with a tea and 'tab-nab'. The elderly kind lady serving watched my lurching and uneven approach as I made heavy going of it. Then, upon my unsteady arrival at the counter, she enquired sympathetically,

"God bless you lad! Have you had a bad accident and hurt your leg?"

"No! I've had a splinter in my finger!" I replied shoving my middle finger up to show her.

Isn't it funny how quickly people can change their nature? For I didn't get my refreshments, but what I did get augmented my knowledge of Liverpool's female foul language rhetoric.

**Around the Buoys**

It's many a long year (1944) since my wartime training at the Gravesend Sea School and admittedly I've passed a lot of water since then, (correction, I've passed over a lot of water since then). But I still harbour guilty feelings over an early morning manoeuvre I was soon inveigled into. Granted, I had a grown-ups body at eighteen, but my brain lagged years behind in the development department making me easily led I suppose.

However, I passed with honours in the grumbling stakes which I soon engaged, for at some absurdly early hour every morning, we were callously roused from our smelly air raid shelter bunks and made to gallop laps around the adjacent sea front gardens. This was to cut us adrift from any lingering home comforts we trainees were still mentally attached to, and also to accustom us to the tough grown up world of seafaring.

## Bill Backshall

Those cold, rainy pitch dark mornings with no nourishment inside us, didn't exactly suggest we elect to run an extra lap of honour, and things didn't improve with the reward at breakfast with a cup of warm brown liquid that was long argued over as being Brown Windsor soup, Bisto gravy, Mahogany wood stain, or a doubtful outsider, coffee. Its true identity remained one of the wars best kept secrets.

After a couple of mornings tiring marathons, things took a dramatic upturn when I was approached by three older lads with a few weeks training behind them. One addressed me in beautifully enunciated correctly modulated Oxford English.

"Orlrite der ladt? Ryew from Livapewl?"

Cleverly, I recognised they were fellow townies.

"Yeh," I replied, wondering what was coming next.

"Yeh, I'm from Bootle."

He turned to his mates and nodded.

"It's alrite Macca we can truss 'im, ee's from Boot Hill."

Enveloping me in ciggie fumes, he then confided,

"Listen wack, just keep dese instructings Barley orlrite? In de morgan dont go chargin off with them dere light brigade fellahs doin' de Grand National thing, just folly us and bring any other Scousers from your class with yew, OK wacker?"

*Around the Buoys*

So next morning under the cover of darkness and with a few more townies for company, we 'Follyed' our three pilots by quietly peeling off from the rear of the throng, who by now were starting their exhausting gallop. Unseen we tiptoed through rhododendrons, scaled a low wall, then trotted up a side street to where a cheerfully lit drop fronted caravan sold tea, coffee, toast, papers etc to people from nearby work places. After a snack, a smoke and a read of the papers we retraced our steps and again unobserved, and looking suitably knackered, re-joined the struggling tail of the exhausted mob on the final thirty yards or so of the last lap.

One morning as we appeared to stagger home to the finishing line, the awaiting Instructor congratulated us as usual.

"Well done men!" and then jokingly added, "You're the light of my life!"

He would have blown a fuse, however, had he known of our short circuit.

*Bill Backshall*

*"Robert.L. Holt "outward for Apapa. Swimming pool still stowed in No Two.*

**SS Robert l Holt**

**aka "Liverpool Yacht"**

**Evening Tide**

**Bound for Nigeria**

**Slow Ahead on Both**

Aboard the SS "Robert L Holt" the temporary swimming pool had at last been erected and topped up. Off the African Coast it was quite a luxury for passengers and officers to have a cooling dip. After hours, the rest of the crew were allowed to have a bash. It was only about 18 foot square, but as I performed my usual awkward 'belly flop' to enjoy a cooling dip, a cynical Johnny C my old shipmate from Gravesend days, commented, "Careful now 'Speedy'! Don't be creating any rough waves!" Embarrassed by being reminded of my old school nickname, I began to sulk as he explained to the rest of the amused deck gang how I earned that particular title of "Speedy."

In 1944 during our three -month course at the school, an Instructor had stepped out of the keyboard flat and being the first mug he met he casually asked me, without any hint of explanation, "Could I swim?" It seemed an innocuous question and surprised, I answered "Yes, a bit," so he noted my name. I had in fact learnt to swim in a neglected part of a Liverpool canal, where speed was secondary to manoeuvring

## Around the Buoys

around submerged old prams, iron beds, cycle wheels and other uncharted marine hazards.

Even though it was still wartime, one Saturday afternoon, to my great surprise, I found myself lined up with a battery of well-muscled eager young men at a local open air baths on the town's crowded Gala day. I'd somehow become an entrant in a swimming race, probably to make the numbers up. At the starting gun I executed my usual crab like belly flop and coughing and spluttering, surfaced some time later. I was surprised to see a great churning and threshing of the water as the other contestants struck off rapidly, striving to reach the other end first. I now employed one of the two strokes I could manage, at first the leisurely side stroke, but cleverly, I then engaged the breast stroke which, though no faster, at least gave me a good view of the swimmers flashing feet and arms which were now thrashing away towards the finishing end.

I comforted myself with the 'tortoise and hare' story, but then, watching the local dignitaries congratulating the breathless winner, I abandoned all hope of contesting the finish. I approached the halfway mark absolutely alone, for even the unplaced stragglers had by now completed the course. Embarrassed, I realised the only way out of the pool was to carry on and reach the finishing end. After the excitement of the sprint race, the cheering spectators had now settled back in their seats and quietened down Suddenly they noticed me, not quite becalmed, but still under way serenely persistent with what they mistook for

British doggedness. My side and breast strokes, though sadly not creating a bow wave were still getting me along 'handsomely', the word old sailors used for 'slowly with care'. I suppose I was comparable to a canvas rigged vessel after a fleet of swift destroyers had left her floundering in their wake.

A worried official seeing me as a possible hazard to starting the next imminent race invited me through his megaphone to 'Get a move on Son!' but I advised him I was already achieving my maximum rate of knots. The spectators as an encouragement now took up the cry of 'Come on Speedy!' (amongst other names to be honest) and reaching into my reserves of strength I persisted until later to a sarcastic but good humoured ovation, I climbed out of the water staggering around like an exhausted marathon runner.

A distinguished gentleman, reeking of whisky, startled and confused by the loud burst of ironic applause, panicked himself into shaking my hands and congratulated me warmly, probably thinking he'd overlooked me either finishing a lap of honour, or of being a winner of some ensuing event he'd overlooked whilst imbibing another wee 'dram.'

With a consoling arm around my shoulder, I was apologetically advised by an embarrassed official, that very sadly he was afraid that some obscure technicality prevented me from being allowed to participate in any further events on the programme. I accepted this ruling with dignity.

Back aboard the "Robert L Holt," Johnny C finished his more

*Around the Buoys*

than colourful description of my Gravesend sea school swimming highlights and to a further burst of ironic applause from the deck gang I climbed out of the ship's tiny pool knowing full well I had been re-christened by all hands. So with the truth out, I might as well sign off as, 'Speedy' Bill Backshall.

**Boat Deck Party**

Aged thirteen, the outbreak of war terminated my elementary schooling. Living alongside the Liverpool docks and already a ship enthusiast, I sought and eventually found employment therein. The whole dockland was full to capacity with vessels of every description sometimes moored two or more abreast undergoing frantic defence alterations etc.

I was enthralled in these surroundings, the sights, smells and sounds of the shipping world, coupled with the nightly bombings made my life very exciting. Seamen, stevedores, riggers, lady cleaners, every type of tradesmen all worked feverishly preparing these ships for another dangerous voyage. The place was alive with bustling humanity.

I assisted an engineer overhauling ship's telegraph system, by removing the wooden panels that covered the wiring/chain/pulleys, etc., and one vessel I worked aboard was the "City of Dieppe" lying in the West Alex' Dock. Parked incongruously on her boat deck awaiting transfer ashore, was a beautifully polished grand piano, a symbol of peacetime luxury, but now in wartime reduced to so much ballast. At dinnertime I lifted the keyboard lid and repeatedly plonked the bass notes of "Boogie-Woogie" with one finger, the extent of my limited repertoire.

An elderly down at heel workman approached, smiling and shaking his head slowly. I cheekily enquired, 'Could he do any better?' He nodded, and I thought scornfully, 'Just as if!' Looking around carefully, as if afraid of being censured by the ships Officers, he perched on the stool and remarked, 'It had always been his ambition to perform on such a wonderful grand piano.'

Flexing his fingers, he started to play slowly, but immediately it became obvious he had been and still remained an accomplished pianist. This puzzled me, for he looked impoverished, and should surely have been in far better circumstances considering his professional standard. His playing soon attracted a growing audience who were enjoying their lunch hour and soon a group of cheery, high spirited lady cleaners were dancing around the boat deck in their heavy aprons and head scarves. They were quickly joined by male partners in boiler suits and overalls.

The old man, smiling now, stepped up the tempo, stepped on the loud pedal and introduced more popular songs. Eventually the whole deck became crowded with happy, smiling work folk encouraging the pianist and dancers with a good old sing song.

*Around the Buoys*

What a welcome safety valve relief it was after nights of sleepless bombing ordeals. All too soon one –o-clock arrived and it was back to the grim realities of wartime, but with spirits greatly cheered and recharged, thanks to an old down at heel dock worker.

Working aboard numerous similar vessels fuelled my sole ambition and eventually I departed from Lime Street station for Gravesend Sea School. I couldn't have been any happier; my dreams had come true, I was going to be a merchant seaman.

At the training barracks, it wasn't a highly polished classy Grand, but an old upright untuned piano that stood in the drill pavilion and though during dinner hours I repeatedly plonked my boogie-woogie notes wistfully, and regularly offered up silent prayers, sadly my old pianist shipmate didn't show up. I didn't think he would really. He'd already fulfilled his ambition whilst I was only preparing to realise mine and anyway, I thought, magical memory moments are always within easy recall, stowed in our precious memories locker.

**Pocket Bottletrip**

Between voyages I would spend time converting my ex "Hinakura" lifeboat shored up alongside the Gladstone Graving dock. Well-meaning ship repairmen would stroll over during their lunch hour to examine my progress, often bearing gifts such as pots of boot topping paint, brushes, brass screws, ropes, handy lengths of timber, ballast, etc. Anything they thought useful. I suspected they were subconsciously paying homage to the Gods of Adventure, secretly hoping one day to escape from their workaday boredom, and set sail with me, leaving the Liver birds astern, bound for Tahiti.

My brother in law, Jimmy volunteered help too. Employed by the Dock Board and dressed in their smart uniform he had a small office just inside the gates of a main dock police check point After many years *of* service he was on first name terms with the eagle eyed policemen, who were adept at preventing stolen goods exiting the dockland. They knew him to be a good hard working man, a church goer, who ran a youth's football team, a scout group, and who organised charities etc. A man known for simply spending his life helping others.

One day Jimmy discovered a drum of marine white gloss paint hidden behind his office, obviously stolen but being difficult to get through the dock gates it was now abandoned by the nervous thieves. True to form he decided to help me knowing a gallon would paint my boat topsides nicely and he conceived a brilliant plan to smuggle enough past the vigilant policemen.

Late afternoon he would refill his now empty milk bottle with the white paint and carefully wiping and refitting the top, he would place it sticking out of his uniform coat pocket, and at five o clock, along with many more homeward bound

*Around the Buoys*

workmen, he would confidently walk out the gate often with a "Goodnight Bob!" or whosoever was on duty.

Things went well at first with the gallon container filling nicely at his home, but walking out the gate on his eighth and final trip, the duty constable shouted to him,

"Jimmy! Could you spare us a little of your Milk?" and pointing to the bottle added,

"We haven't got a drop and we're dying for a cuppa."

Jimmy was now torpedoed amidships and forced into engaging a hurried damage limitation programme.

"There's a spare half pint back in my office Bob, I'll get it for you!" He spluttered going about and retracing his steps quickly to avoid further engagement. Luckily, there was a half pint, but it belonged to, and was stowed in his absent colleague's locker. Taking a heavy screwdriver he burst the door open thinking, *'I'll need to do some serious apologising tomorrow.'* Walking out of the gate again with an assumed casual air, he handed the half bottle to the constable saying,

"There's plenty in there Bob, you're welcome."

It was only then he noticed the broadest of grins on the Police Sergeants face who was standing some yards away and who now shouted over,

"Thanks Jimmy! It's probably fresher than that bottle in your pocket!" and waving Jimmy through the gate, he added loudly, "I think that one's gone off. I can smell it from over here!"

The milk run was over, and anyway, as a teetotaller Jimmy never did like one 'over the eight.'

**Hat Trick**

Propped against the bitts, Ginger and I sat looking at the ships in the Gladstone Dock, and despite my mate having a full discharge book he could still boast a shock of rusty hair. Anyway, there's one thing about looking at ships, you don't need to be conversational, you just sort'a feel them with your eyes, it's kinda nice and restful.

Looming overhead was the stern of a large cargo vessel and inscribed on it was the usual name and port of registration, that is, if you could understand the damned thing for this one was in a foreign language and I head-shakingly remarked,

"It's distinctly indecipherable."

Ginger worked the pipe to the side of his mouth, "Not only that Bill, you can't even read the bloody thing."

Flying from the poop was a huge ensign with a gold hammer and sickle on a red background. After a spell Ginger removed his pipe, spat in the dock, and croaked knowingly, "Ruskie."

"Well gerraway!" I replied sarcastically and left it at that

*Around the Buoys*

A smartly dressed man carrying a small case hurried down the quay worriedly checking on a sheet of paper. Glancing up at the bows and then the bridge, he shook his head, and looking puzzled, walked aft to check the writing on the stern. Still nonplussed, he then addressed we two loafers,

"What the hell's the name of this vessel men?"

"Blowed if we know Chief, how the hell can anyone read those foreign hydraulics? But I can tell you this, she's singled up ready to sail!"

"Thanks Ginger," he unerringly fastened on the correct nickname and smiling added,

"Yes, I thought so, she's my job. I'm the Pilot booked to take her out, but God knows how we're supposed to identify some of these foreign vessels!" Off he stamped to climb the steep gangway.

"Best reef your topsails Pilot, it's getting very squally!" Shouted my mate, ever helpful with free marine advice. A raised hand acknowledged receipt of the weather report.

The shore gang now moved us on from the bitts ready to cast off, so we sauntered amidships to watch the rest of the entertainment. Whistles whistled, windlasses winched, tugs tugged and with the vessel easing off the quay, came a mega phoned order, "Leggo the spring," and suddenly peering down at us from the wing of the bridge was the Pilot. Spotting us he waved, "If I'm taking the wrong vessel to sea, I'm blaming you two men!" He joked.

Another head appeared obviously the Russian Captain curious about the laughter. Unfortunately, as he leaned over a sudden gust dislodged his large red starred uniform cap sending it spinning. It arced gracefully down towards us where Ginger, by some stroke of luck, plucked it instinctively from the air, and though the ship was now 2 or 3 yards off the quay, he pitched it back aboard shouting, "Here's your Sputnik back Cap'n!"

Shore gang, crew and even the stoney faced Captain smiled and applauded what looked like a music hall act, and an admiring Pilot bawled,

"Ginger, I found out she's called the 'Red Saviour,' and the Skipper's just remarked she was probably named after you!!"

**West Gladstone Wall**

As a boy I delighted in watching the ships

That steamed past the West Gladstone Wall

No sight struck me finer than an outward bound liner

Before these containers and all

Furness and Elders, the great C P R

Blue Funnel, Cunard, plus the stylish Blue Star

Yes, I recognised each shipping line

*Around the Buoys*

At flood time departing and handsomely starting

Those voyages now in decline

Yes, my interest bounded for Romance surrounded

A tramp clearing Waterloo beach

Where was she bound, what port would be found

On her wandering voyaging reach?

Could it be Accra or Auckland or Dakar

Or trading the Chilean Coast?

Geelong or Hong Kong or Halifax freezing

Or the 'Perishing Gulf' where you roast?

But the West Gladstone Wall no longer sees all

Those old liners and tramps sad to say

But Gravesend gave us a chance

To be part of Romance

Of an Era that's ours to recall

*Bill Backshall*

**Red Lips**

I've gorra confess I've joined the old dreamers

Still livin' in the days of the smokey stacked steamers.

Whose hulls were plain black with odd red lead patches

And derricks that swung over five or six hatches.

When liners looked like they just aught to do.

Their well-designed liveries made them pleasant to view.

Today's styles are different. I'll accept with a smile

That vessels of the day had a modern box style.

What turned me sarcastic and then filled me with rancour

When I saw a cruise liner boasting eyes near the anchor.

To make matters worse, please believe me, I caught a

Sight of red lips where the bows cut the water.

Let go the cook's trousers. I've seen it all now.

Two eyes at the anchor, luscious lips on the prow.

Perhaps thy'll go further, paint two ears on the stack.

Will the arse end be split with two cheeks at the back?

*Around the Buoys*

Lord, what are they doing.

Such ships look bizarre.

Thank God I've reached eight bells.

Roll on Crossin' the Bar

### Name Calling

Perhaps you know the run, Freetown, Takoradi, Apapa, up the Creeks to Sapele to discharge, and then on down the coast and up the Congo to Matardi. It was there the Bosun told me I was to be night watchman. No big deal for I couldn't see anything exciting about going ashore in that particular place. The job was a soft touch really, checking the moorings between dozes, the river having a very strong current.

The first night was uneventful, but on the second about 11pm, one of the A.B's came staggering aboard half shot, gasping to me,

"Bill, get aboard that 'Coconut Palm' lying astern of us. The Mate is there in the mess room with a full bottle of whisky to crack! He's looking for company to chat to."

This seemed very unusual, a Chief Officer in the mess drinking whisky, willing to socialise with deck hands, so I beetled along and sure enough there he sat all alone looking half shot.

"Sit down son and have a bash," he invited.

I settled in and the first thing I queried after a liberal swig was,

"How come a Chief Mate is slumming it with deck hands, surely that's unheard of?"

"No," he slurred, "the sailors are Nigerians aboard this ship, so I can't relate to them socially. Actually, I started like you, a deck hand, but by studying I came up through the hawse pipe to my present position. Occasionally it's nice to swing the lamp and reminisce with ordinary deck hands after being among Empire Builders and the other Officer's, who often get to be boring, anyway drink up."

I didn't refuse. We chatted for quite some time about things with me doing most of the drinking till the whisky got on soundings. Then it started to embolden me and I said,

"I don't like the name of your vessel, Coconut Palm!"

And I quoted some of the lovely names of RN ships, such as the 'Indomitable', the 'Illustrious', the 'Indefatigable' the 'Formidable' etc.

Nearly out of the game, he managed to retort rather testily,

"So what? I didn't want to be the Mate on an aircraft carrier. Anyway, what about the name of your vessel? It's not so hot either."

*Around the Buoys*

He finally sprawled on the table with a broad grin on his face and started to snore gently. I couldn't understand what was so funny.

I finished off the remains and decided to get back aboard my own vessel, but on taking a few steps along the quay the drink suddenly took charge and my senses started reeling so badly I had to fight to keep myself conscious for my steering gear was malfunctioning as I staggered drunkenly along, very concerned about the rivers strong current a few yards to my right. I just about made it up the gangway, but immediately collapsed on the deck.

Hours later, the Kroo night watchman woke me and dragged me forward to the focsul where I spent the rest of the morning sleeping. Wakening, I thought about the Mates curious words "Your ships name's not so hot either, and that's no shit you must agree."

By the way, I was serving aboard one of Elder Dempster's, the M.V. **Onitshu.**

**Stirring It Up**

After any drunken behaviour in harbour, the Mate may spitefully order the Bosun to break out the chipping hammers as starters for a head-achey day or two. Then to follow that, he could of course have the stays, shrouds and runner's fish oiled a nasty smelly job.

Next he may play his master card and decide to have the topmasts painted, so when the Bosun appears armed with a gantline and chair that will be the signal for most of the A.B's to quietly disperse to lowly populated parts of the vessel, the fiddly, lazareete, chain locker, etc. on secretive errands.

When he throws the chair and gantline at an unsuspecting you, it means you've won first prize. Once perilously hoisted up there, it's best not to look down, you'll not only feel nervous, but also see the fathoms of unpainted mast stretching below. Once started, do a good job on the mast side facing the bridge, for bored Officers with nothing else to do will spend hours "holiday hunting" your work with binoculars.

Don't bother too much about the other side nobody will see this part, nor climb up there just to have a look. A definite advantage with this task is that with practice, and by judging wind allowance, by catching a fully loaded brush against the chair, a fine spray of paint droplets can be directed deckwards onto any passing member of the crew. This will be recognised as an accident for no one can blame a man busily working away so high.

Covering a Chief Steward with droplets requires great patience, for they are known to have the cunning of a fox, but if successful, your esteem is greatly enhanced with the rest of the crowd until pay-off day. Other crew members sprayed are rated by a handicap system with galley and deck boys counting only as practice.

*Around the Buoys*

There are no known records of a Cook being paint sprayed. It is widely agreed that seeing the Cook on deck at sea causes unrest and is considered to be an omen of Bad Luck, especially among 'Old Shellbacks'. Sighting a mermaid, viewing the Liver Birds after a long voyage, or running aground, only things of that calibre will encourage his appearance. He will be easily recognised by his pasty white face, his prickly heat rash, and by his brave smile as he blinks continually, unaccustomed to even to even the weakest of sunshine.

When the top masts are completed, it is accepted the AB concerned can now pose at the foot of the boat deck ladder enjoying the admiration of female passengers impressed by his bravery, little realising he's been scared witless from the moment he was hoisted, and is even now sorry he didn't join the Army where they don't have silly things like masts sticking up everywhere. As a reward, the Bosun will now give him a nice fleet of boat deck bulkheads to paint, generally where the said Lady passengers take afternoon tea'.

The rest of the deck crowd who have by now returned from their far flung journeys whistling casually and feigning disappointment at the job having been done without their knowledge, will get the awkward deck head banjo fleets to soogie or paint.

*Bill Backshall*

**On the Fiddle**

For wartime conscription purposes, aged seventeen and along with many more bewildered young men, I was examined by half a dozen Doctors in a city hall and suspiciously declared A1. The doctor who examined my eyes wore bottle top lenses in his own glasses and apparently overlooked my poor vision.

Eventually I was able to attend the Gravesend sea school and start a seagoing life. Though at times I was worried about my poor vision on look-out and wheel duties, I never hit any other ships nor ran a vessel aground, though I once mistakenly reported some low lying clouds as Madagascar and a whale as a U boat. "Bloody wars over now Son," the Mate growled.

Steering through the Suez Canal was a drag, especially at night time with that searchlight on the bows and those little white markers to guide you. During one particular transit I did three continuous hours night steering, making my eyes rather bleary and probably contributing to the following accident.

Preparing for the oncoming watch I had just filled the large lidless teapot with scalding water when I misjudged placing it on the table and knocked it against the fiddle that runs around the edge. The contents splashed over my right hip and down my thigh. Wearing only shorts and brothel creepers it hurt agonisingly causing me to do a sort of Highland fling much to the amusement of the onlookers who

*Around the Buoys*

applauded my performance. I eventually soaked a towel and kept flushing cold water over the area to relieve the pain whilst the watch were very patient and only complained half-heartedly about the loss of their brew.

Later the Chief Steward called carrying an important but dusty medical book and said, a little nonplussed, "I'll have to look the treatment up!" then he added regretfully, "It's a pity you didn't break your leg or have a dose of the crabs, I've treated them complaints before."

Next day frighteningly large water filled blisters appeared hanging down over the scald but looking more like balloons than blisters. The crew kindly visited the focsul to ogle at them, some prodding them, some photographing them, and some offering to autograph them.

Worryingly, the Cook joined in the pilgrimage to enjoy the unusual entertainment and of course this caused an upset it being considered a bad omen seeing the Cook on deck. Only things with the calibre of running aground, being torpedoed, or paying off generally make a Cook appear. I recognised him by his pasty face, by him scratching his 'prickly heat' rash, and by his shy smile as he blinked rapidly being unused to even the weakest of sunshine. He offered me some lotion which I carefully didn't rub anywhere near the area, as he kindly explained,

"S'for me rash!"

Shortly after the incident, as if by magic, the blisters suddenly disappeared overnight leaving the skin all pink and fresh, like new. The Chief Steward, suddenly remembering his Patient, called to the focsul and triumphantly announced,

"I've got it cracked lad! Splash cold water over them, and keep them covered loosely!"

"You're a little bit adrift Chief," I apologised, feeling I'd let the side down, adding "The blisters are gone, and the skins brand new again now!" Examining the new skin he looked disappointed and slamming shut his medical book he stamped off without a word. However, I overheard him complaining to the Bosun at the focsul entrance.

"Impatient and inconsiderate sods these Liverpool lads."

**Football Pool**

Returning home after another long tramping voyage made me realise my street corner buddies has by now either married off, or had shipped out themselves. We'd spent our youthful days there listening to older men between trips blowing about adventures in B.A, New York, Bombay, etc., whetting our ambitions. But with the corner now occupied by a younger different breed of men, I no longer fitted in.

Being single I hadn't reached the stage where some married men, after being home for a spell and with the household finances now in shallow water, find their dinner consisting of a cup of tea and their discharge book offered on a plate, a subtle reminder to get back to sea again. Best get myself down to the 'Pool was my solution too, realising a seafarers life, apart from his family , can become quite lonely at home after a few long voyages. Picking up the threads of the past isn't easy, so I visited Paradise Street and manoeuvring past the flotsam of similar unemployed deck hands, fire bobbies, Cunard Yanks and drifters; I queued at the Pool counter. Surprisingly, the clerk ushered me in and offered my rent book to a Chief Mate.

He didn't exactly study it like it was a best seller, for being an O/S there was only my Gravesend discharge and three VGs in it. Shanghaied on long voyages was a crafty maritime ploy to keep me out of their way I thought. He threw it aside indifferently like it was entitled "Origami in the Outer Hebrides" or some such boring read, then with a worried look he fired a question. Nothing seamanlike such as 'Could I steer?' or make 'A fancy Turks head?' or 'Splice a dog's dick?' Oh no! Quite seriously he asked me, "Can you play football?"

Surprised and embarrassed, the shipping clerk gave a cover up cough and tried to look as if it was an accepted seafaring question, "Yes Sir!" I replied, (I'd been dropped from my school team regularly). "Right! You've got a job!" smiled the Mate looking as pleased as if I'd replied I'd played for Liverpool F.C. "She's the 'John Holt' signing in the morning at the West Queens dock, and more importantly, don't forget your boots!"

In Apapa we played an important grudge match against a

local Nigerian Team, and with our 2$^{nd}$ steward blowing for tugs towards the end of a 2/2 drawing match, and with no one else available, I was reluctantly sent on as a substitute.

Spotting our team running towards our opponent's goal, I thought I'd best join them, but en route pestered by a nasty tsetse fly, I tripped and fell awkwardly. An opposing defender stumbled over my outstretched leg and accidentally kicked the ball against my foot, making it rebound towards their goal. Their goal keeper, attacked by the same tsetse was too distracted swatting the damned thing to prevent the ball glancing off his arse and finishing up in the net.

I was congratulated by my shipmates, convinced I'd scored the winning goal by determination and masterly technique. I made six trips on the 'John Holt' basking in the reflected glory of that fluke goal.

**A Small Silver Badge**

I found my old sea box, stowed away in the shed

It took me back seafaring, (Well, at least in my head).

I brushed off the cobwebs and blew off the dust.

A mouldy smell hit me; still I knew that I must

See the contents from long ago, some falling to bits

Like a passport for 'Alex' and some old pay-off slips.

*Around the Buoys*

Prompting flash backs of voyages board rusty tramp ships.

My Gravesend class photo, the year? 1944,

Brought a lump to my throat, quickly rummaged for more

A certificate boasted "Proof of Gunnery Course"

And a torn manual page where I tried to learn Morse.

Then a beautiful seashell from Tahiti's blue seas

And some snaps of an Albatross mast heading the breeze

Then a photo of we deck hands stripped with tropical tans.

Caught painting the funnel (cutting in two red bands).

A small three part Turks Head knot I'd made on a line

Of round sennet I'd been taught from a shipmate of mine

Then that letter from Marie bored at home, read "Goodbye,"

Giving me the old 'Heave ho', (She married some rich guy!)

Don't tell me you've never had, such things from your past

Stowed away which by chance you unearth at long last.

Like me you're not sure whether to laugh or to cry.

They remind you a great time in life's passed you by.

Well the last thing I fished from that tin box that day

Was a small silver badge, do you remember the way

We wore it with pride? Sadly, now a vague dream,

But there's one thing for certain, tomorrow I mean

To salvage that badge, have it re-burnished bright.

It's a symbol of seafaring that enhanced my young life.

**Left Hook**

At one stage of my life I belonged to a section of people I now dislike, namely 'inflexible know-it-all's'. Those days I would arrogantly dismiss anything I didn't believe in as complete nonsense, but now I realise it's best not to close your mind completely against even the most absurd and unlikely possibilities, I'll tell you why I'm agin' being dogmatic.

During retirement, whilst messing about on my converted ex "Hinakura" steel lifeboat, engine problems forced me into moving the boat, now named "Marlin", in the Leeds & Liverpool canal, from its mooring to the club slipway, 4/5 hundred yards away, where I could better effect repairs.

Preparing for the move I heard a curious tap, tap, tapping coming from the stern. Looking over the after end, I saw to my pleasant surprise, a brand new wooden boat hook floating in the water, the breeze and current causing the alloy hooked end to knock against the metal hull. Obviously it

*Around the Buoys*

had been lost overboard from a passing craft. This was a good find, for my own amateurish boat hook was an ex railway shunter's pole, thick, rough and unsightly with a squiggly metal end that I had found and since used from when my craft was in the Liverpool docks.

It had sufficed for these past three/four years, but now here was a proper quality accessory which looked far more purposeful and seamanlike. I fished my find out, cleaned it up and proudly placed it in the chocks atop the cabin, then taking the old superfluous shunter's pole, I casually threw it, illegally I admit, into the canal murmuring "Fair exchange is no robbery!"

After shoulder-hauling the boat the considerable distance to the slipway past dozens of other members boats, I secured and covered her, then departed for home planning to return at the weekend and carry out the engine repair work.

On Sunday morn, down by the head with spanners, sockets, spark plugs, etc. I arrived to have a bash at the work, but sensibly, being a stickler for important things first, I made a cup of tea and sat mentally preparing for the task.

It was whilst sitting quietly I heard a familiar faint tap, tap, tapping again coming from the arse end. Curious, and with a few hairs misbehaving on the back of my neck, I walked aft and peeped into the water. There, unbelievably, was my old shunter's pole having somehow over the week drifted down stream past the many moored craft and was now weakly knocking with its metal squiggly end on the stern of the

"Marlin" as if exhausted with its efforts. It now lay there seemingly appealing to me for succour.

Considering the multitude of places where it could have finished up, how strange I thought, that it had picked on its old home the "Marlin", where we now lay berthed, and also it was even tapping on the exact spot the new boathook had selected. Inexplicable!!

I stood gawping with my past dogmatic beliefs in disarray, eerily knowing coincidence was a poor excuse, tears welled in my eyes as I realised how callously and disloyally I had treated it after all the good service it had given me over the years. Shamefaced I leaned over the gunwale and rescued it from the watery grave I had casually abandoned it too. Guiltily, and to make amends, I cleaned it thoroughly and placed it in the chocks starboard side, with the newly found one port side, hoping they would enjoy that arrangement. It was only then I felt I could look the boating world in the face once again.

I swear the basics of this story are true, but as I've mentioned earlier, I never believed in such things as crop circles, fairies, UFOs, devils or stories of other forms of intelligence. But now I've opened my mind to a little more belief, recalling an old L/Pool shipmate's saying,

### ***Bobby's Baton's Halter Faces and Circumstances Halters Cases.***

*Around the Buoys*

**Rough Passage**

A quick peck on the cheek as Ma wished me "God-Bye Son, Take Care," and humping my sea bag I made my way through the early morning rain to Seaforth station, the northern terminus of the old Overhead railway many years ago. I was re-joining the SS 'John Holt' for a four month voyage to the West Coast of Africa as a deck hand. Neither the healthiest, nor the most glamorous of trips. In fact the coast was once known as the 'White Man's Grave', so the shipping line to encourage the crews loyalty, gave each man his own tiny cabin plus 10% atop his wages by way of an inducement.

First though, I needed to get to the Queens Dock to join her, and boarding the wooden three coached train during the morning peak hour, I prepared myself mentally and physically for the rough but exciting passage. These coaches were known disrespectfully but cheerfully, as the "Orange boxes" by local children through their orange colour cast, and wooden box shape.

The train soon filled to capacity with every type of rain drenched workmen, office clerks, tradesmen, stevedores, porters, painters, scalers, seamen, lady cleaners etc., with quite a number burdened with various pieces of marine related equipment, machinery, ropes, painting gear, tool boxes, large wooden patterns, instruments, anything portable and mainly under repair, all were dragged into the coaches disregarding the comfort of the already sardine packed passengers, each person determined to get to their own destination.

Soon the visibility was down to a few feet with the thick blue haze of tobacco smoke and the steamy atmosphere making station identification difficult. In the selected carriages if the "No Smoking" signs had been written in Swahili, they couldn't have been anymore disregarded. For folk unable to unable to see the station titles through the muggy atmosphere and choking blue smoke, men with window berths would helpfully call the names at each stop. "Gladstone", "Canada", "Bramley-Moore", "Wapping", "Toxteth", "Herculaneum", lovely names as good sounding as the vessels titles that could be viewed berthed in those docks, "Samaria", "Empress of Britain", "Herdsman", "Sydney Star", "Turkistan", "Automedon" etc.

During the run, lost looking Lascar and other foreign seamen would be questioned as to the name of the ship and then directed and helped off at their correct dock. As quickly as some folk fought their way off the train at their desired stations, others similarly burdened, stormed aboard. "Tons of room here!" would be the optimistic cry as they charged the doorways with the patient already tightly packed people at the back giving ground as wooden patterns, and tool boxes were used as battering rams.

The old wooden coaches heavily laden, would creak and groan like a sailing ship in heavy weather as they lurched and tilted dangerously at the Alex' Dock bend in the track, or when speeding up alarmingly as the train careered downwards, then upwards at the low level Bramley-Moore Dock and onwards to the Pier Head and South end docks. Finally reaching my destination the Brunswick Dock station, I gratefully struggled my gear onto the platform and recognising a fellow shipmate also alighting we gave one another the thumbs up sign, and relieved, we sniggered as we quoted the old seaman's headshaking humorous remark, "Well that's the roughest part of the voyage over!!"

**Chay's War**

In the early days of that vaguely remembered WW2 my brother Chay followed my eldest brother's example and volunteered for the R N. After training, he told me he 'interfered' with mine laying and mine sweeping in the North Sea.

He escaped an enemy machine gunning but later with the stern end of his trawler being blown up he finished up with an injury to his leg, and with a stroke of exceptional kindness by an Admiralty officer, he was drafted for a short period to a small trawler at the Pier Head, Liverpool, mainly to 'exasperate' as he put it, ('recuperate' as they put it.) Chay maintained it was a secret agreement between the Krieg marine and the R N to get him out of the way, so both sides could continue the war in a sensible manner.

The small Belgian fisherman he was attached to, the "Rodger Blonde," with another craft the "Jan Virginia" had escaped the German invasion of their country and with some members of their family still aboard had arrived at the extreme end of the Liverpool landing stage.

Occasionally they transported small marine barrage balloons to vessels lying at anchor in the Mersey. These balloons were designed to prevent enemy aircraft from low level strafing and dive bombing vulnerable shipping, but though useful, they weren't very pivotal in the war's fortunes.

After enjoying the visits to his local home whilst stationed at the Pier Head, the Admiralty decided to ship him to Anzio, Italy where, according to Chay, the situation soon went adrift but he refused to accept any responsibility. Finally, he finished up at Bari a Southern Italian port, which was falsely regarded as pretty safe from attack. The port was being used as a main supply base for the English and American armies who were now progressing well into Northern Italy. These supplies were that important, brilliant lights were being used at night time to facilitate discharging the cargoes. Over confidence reigned and caution was being thrown to the wind. It has also been suggested that additional harbour lights were switched on from the local power station on the night in question by unknown sympathisers.

An enemy reconnaissance plane flying high over the busy port, had earlier reported back about the vulnerability of the target and German steps were taken to attack. 2 Dec 1943. A hundred Junker 88's made a surprise night raid on the port and sank 17 large cargo vessels, badly damaging 30 or so more.

*Around the Buoys*

The port remained closed for many weeks throwing the Allies war machine out of major action for a considerable length of time, a tremendous blow to the Allied cause. After the war, Chay reckoned that if he had taken the "Roger Blonde" out there with her barrage balloon, the losses would have been negligible.

**Tobacco Trade**

The vessel was diverted from Antofagasta to Iquique on the Chilean coast, and most of us had never heard of this place before and no wonder, for it was only a smallish port but still with quite a few vessels lying off at anchor loading what I found out was Nitrate which smelt like iodine to me. The whole area including what I took to be the Andes in the far distant background, was barren, and some focsul lawyer spouted they hadn't had rain here for twenty odd years, which I could easily believe.

Soon we were loading the peculiar smelling white fertiliser which was bound for Egypt, with part cargo en route for the States, whilst we deck hands had eyes bound for the jetty with a sense of thirstiness, but the Master had us well clocked and subbed us a few 'potatoes' or pesos or whatever they called them.

Taking a small motor boat ferry that was laid on to service all the ships at anchor, we made it ashore and spread out around the town rubber necking and having a few drinks etc.

Later, mustered on the quay for our return aboard, Johnny my shipmate, told the gathered crew it was my 19th birthday, and all hands then had a tarpaulin muster with whatever odd few pesos they had left and told me to take it and go back and have a few more drinks to celebrate, which I did in the first bar.

It was there I met 'Blanca Rosa' a nice girl who spoke just a little English and realising my funds were very limited she led me by the hand to a tiny corrugated iron roofed cinema where she smiled and pointed to the placard which read "The Four Feathers" the splendid English movie, with subtitles in Spanish.

It was very enjoyable and at the end of the film the small audience stood and clapped and cheered the movie with great spirit. Blanca Rosa then shouted something in Spanish and pointed to me, and they then cheered me as well. I bowed and waved graciously not sure of why I warranted a burst of applause. Maybe they thought I was one of those brave English soldiers.

She accompanied me back to the departure wharf and with a little peck on the cheek bid me 'Adios'. I'm afraid that was the end of my Chilean romance, and I nipped aboard the little ferry launch bound for my vessel. There must have been a dozen or more seafarers like myself en route to their different ships, and various languages could be heard, just like the United Nations on a day out. One by one each ship was visited with the complement of our craft growing smaller.

## Around the Buoys

I was getting a little impatient for apparently my vessel was last on the list. Finally, we were bound for the next to last one leaving just we two passengers. The other guy, obviously to break the silence, turned to me and asked "Speaka da Inglish, Amigo?" The American clocked me as some sort of Dago. "Too true, Yank I should do, I live there." I smiled, and he burst out laughing. "Sorry Fellah I didn't know you were a Limey!"

Well, we got chatting and he knew Liverpool well, sailing there with the United States Line. He enquired about things in the 'Caradoc' and how was Lime Street? Then finding it was my birthday, he wished me a "Happy Birthday!" and presented me with a large cigar. Truthfully, I didn't fancy the thing, but with him holding a lighter for me, I reluctantly took a deep drag or two and immediately started to cough my heart up, but disguising the severity I managed to splutter, "Gee. Thanks a lot, Buddy, this sure is a fine cigar and I'm certainly going to enjoy it."

Luckily we had arrived at his vessel now and I gave him a wave of appreciation as he climbed aboard. But the cigar smoke and taste was damn near killing me and as the launch pulled away, I quickly threw it overboard into the drink, cursing the bloody thing. Glancing up I'm pretty sure he had spotted me and was having a secret laugh.

Later in the trip saw our freighter in Baltimore, and taking an early evening, stroll, I was stopped by a well-dressed guy who apologized for interrupting my walk, but he said he originally came from England many years ago and overhearing my accent had made him nostalgic, especially when he saw me pulling out my Wild Woodbine cigarette packet (A very cheap make, popular at home in those days). "My, how I'd like to enjoy one," he said, "just to take me back all those years ago in England when I was a boy starting to smoke."

"Sure thing," I agreed, offering him one of my 'Woodies', "I'm only too happy to oblige." Smiling, he took it and lit up taking a deep drag, and after another deep puff, he started to cough his heart up. Finally, able to talk, he gasped "My word I really am going to enjoy this old Woodbine," and then quickly saying, "Thanks a lot Buddy," he was away at a fast rate of knots around the street corner. Amused, I carefully peeped around and watched him throw the thing down in disgust mumbling to the skies, "God damned thing near killed me!!"

'Payback time,' as they say in the United States.

**My Irish Mate**

'Precipitation', the weatherman called it. I called it something more descriptive and distasteful, for preparing the "Jonathan" for sailing resulted in my being drenched with the non-stop November downpour.

Allowed a quick visit home, I squelched up Church Street, for circumstances dictated my transport would be the dock road bus, which was carefully timed to wear very little tarmac

## Around the Buoys

away with its frequency schedule. The immediate area was earmarked for redevelopment with most buildings derelict, so reaching the main road knowing the bus stop was coverless, I sheltered in the doorway of a boarded up corner shop ready to make a dash upon my transports arrival, (any day now I thought sarcastically.) Waiting, I trawled for that vaguely remembered poem "November"-

"No sun, No moon, no morn, no noon, no dawn, no dusk. November."

The rain and darkness, plus the dreary surroundings were so disheartening that eventually I burst out laughing at the bloody misery of it all. "Stuff You!" I shouted in cheerful defiance, sticking my fingers up at the Liverpool gloom, safe in the knowledge I'd soon be in "flying fish weather." Pulling my sodden overcoat collar tighter around my neck kept out gusts that invaded the doorway hell bent on trickling down and wetting any remaining dry parts of my shirt.

A sudden splash of cheerful light across the road indicated 3pm closing time at the only decent building around, the Derby pub. The now wedged open door invited the customers to leave, whilst disclosing the pleasant bright interior. "I'm just in time to be too damned late for a pint and a warm meal," I cursed.

The patrons trundled out battening down their waterproof's as they departed in various directions. Eventually the last customer rolled out, singing a soft Irish lullaby, accompanied by the comforting chink of bottles in his pockets.

He veered to starboard and heaved to before settling on a course for the Alex' Dock. He wore a jauntily angled mariner's peaked cap and the top coat thrown casually over his shoulders disclosed three gold rings around the cuffs. Paint splashed flannels confessed he wasn't the Mate of some smart cargo-liner, but probably a coaster. Cheered by his happiness I then dismissed him from my thoughts and returned to my look-out duty. Nothing on the horizon, but I kept focussed as though this would encourage the damned bus to materialise.

Suddenly I became aware of a close presence, the reek of drink immediately suggesting it was my Irish Mate. Then a tug on my pocket occurred. Turning, I became aware that he had dropped silver coins into my pocket murmuring "God Bless ye Son" and was now once more dock bound.

Taken aback, it was too late to explain I wasn't on the beach, desperately in need, but anyway, that would have negated his kindness. I could only think to shout "Thanks Chief!" a little guiltily. He never answered, never turned his head, just continued his under way lullaby.

He had clocked me with my collar pulled up tight as a drenched, hungry, homeless, down on my luck drifter, and had worked me a substantial handout without hesitation. He wanted no thanks, he gave me no song and dance lecture about "Getting myself work", he wanted no phoney media publicity trumpeting how generous he was, he preached no advisory sermon, just quietly worked me a seafarer's life-belt, then... Finito.

*Around the Buoys*

I doubt he ever gave me another thought, but through my many years his act of compassion floats often and strongly to the surface from my memories locker, reminding me of the lesson I learned about practical kindness without conditions

**Stern Light View**

Joining the M.V. "Sekondi" at Tilbury, I learnt that during the last voyage, the Captain had disappeared at sea, presumed lost overboard. Accidents such as that are thankfully rare and inclined to happen more so at night time on cargo vessels often through rough weather.

Another possibility is that, mid ocean, right forward, and alone on 'Look-out' duty in the wee small hours can become very boring with nothing to report hour after hour and night after night. This can be relieved by entertaining thoughts of home, and in calm weather by leaning over the forrad rails dreamily watching the prow cutting through the water producing the continual boiling and ever changing phosphorescent bow waves.

During this fascinating diversion though, a mixture of drowsiness and slight hypnotism caused by wave watching, can induce an involuntary "nod off" for a second or two, or maybe longer. With a start you suddenly regain control of your thoughts and pull back, realising you've neglected your duty and worse, you could quite easily have tumbled overboard with not a soul being aware, until the next "Lights are bright!" report, or your relief finds you missing. Shocked, you guiltily resolve to remain more alert. As the "Sekondi" tragedy and the following report confirm, this frightening accident of falling overboard can happen to any member of the crew.

1957 and the vessel, the S.S. "British Monarch" having transited the Panama Canal was now bound for Japan. One morning Stan Mc Nally the Radio Operator noticed the Second Mate's early morning cup of tea was untouched and he had not attended breakfast. Concerned, Stan began an intense search and it became obvious Dough Wardrop was missing. In fact, he had accidentally fallen overboard coming off watch at four am. When the Captain was informed the ship was immediately put about and the almost impossible task of trying to find the Second Mate began.

At noon, after ploughing the reverse course the vessel approached the hopefully estimated position of the accident. The Master and Mate now carefully decided to alter course by a few degrees to starboard compensating for drift. The second Mate's life was now in his shipmates hands with this gamble. Everyone not on watch manned look out positions, with all eyes desperately searching for a tiny bobbing head in the vast Pacific Ocean, and one hour later an excited lookout shouted "Man in the water off the starboard bow!" and sure enough it was the Second Mate waving furiously.

A boat was lowered to pick him up and he had enough strength to climb aboard a rope ladder although once aboard he collapsed immediately. It was a miraculous recovery because only for the Radio Officers alertness and the slight course adjustment, there's no doubt he would never have been found. Later, Doug said he knew he would be missed at breakfast and believed he would be back aboard for lunch.

He was right and it is comforting to know that miracles do happen. But a timely warning to other seafarers should you ever be unfortunate enough to have a fish eye view of the stern light fast disappearing towards the horizon, I wouldn't rely too heavily upon them happening too often.

**Crossed Lines**

Though that damned WW2 was well over, surprisingly folk seemed reluctant to discuss or refer to it, they'd sort of gloss it over, almost as if it hadn't happened. Subconsciously, I suppose they were trying to bury the pain of the thing. However, even years later 'Ginger' never got over it, but you could understand that considering his past experiences, getting the 'hammer' twice, once on a tanker, and again on a cargo vessel, seeing some of his shipmates dying or doomed.

Those occasions kept bubbling to the surface with him at the slightest suggestion. It happened again as we strolled down the Queens Dock quay heading back to E.D's old vessel S. S. "Biafra" during our dinner hour. We were surprised suddenly by a shout of "Tommy!" coming from behind, and turning we saw a small German diesel coaster had crept up on us quietly, ready to berth just ahead of us. A deck hand had a heaving line ready and he signalled he wanted us to catch it and then pull the bow mooring line ashore to slip over the bitts.

A larger vessel would have had a shore gang ready, but in this case they were relying upon somebody handy to help out. It was no problem and like a seaman or docker in any port would do, we grabbed the mooring rope safely and then I coiled the heaving line and threw it back aboard as we slowly walked up the quay to where the bitts were.

Suddenly I heard Ginger mumbling and cursing, "I'm sure that's the "B----d! He's got the same hooked nose." Puzzled I asked him, "What are you on about Ginger?"

"I'm sure that's the fellah in the uniform watching us, who

was on that bleedin' U Boat that sunk us!" Adding, "It came right alongside our lifeboat asking if our Captain was aboard, but we cracked on ignorance saying, 'No, we think he went down with her!'"

Then he repeated, "Yes I'm bloody sure that's the fellah there, him with the hooked nose who asked us about the Skipper".

"No, it won't be," I said, trying to console him. "That was years ago and it's too much of a coincidence." But Ginger continued to curse and swear glaring at the uniformed guy who could plainly see and hear something was amiss.

As we threw the bight over the bitts the deck hand shouted a grateful "Danke!" But the Officer with the two rings still looked upset, especially when he heard Ginger pointedly referring to him with, "I'd like to knock your f------ block off!" The uniform guy strode over towards us and spoke directly to Ginger, "What's the problem 'Scouse'. I'm from Crosby and to get a handy lift back home D B S from Hamburg where I was in Hospital with what they thought was a heart attack, I bummed a quick passage back on this vessel."

"Told yer so!" I sneered at Ginger, feeling very self-righteous, the way you do when you've been proved 100% right. Aboard the "Biafra", Ginger, still reluctant to be in the wrong, later suggested,

"Think he could be in disguise?"

**Gravesend Passport**

Attendance at Gravesend Sea School guaranteed a magical passport. Melbourne, Aden, Panama, Bombay etc., becoming common sights through the porthole. However seafarers eventually become blasé arriving at such ports disdaining to throw even a casual look, Freetown or Fremantle, what did it matter? But once in a while, especially aboard cargo seeking tramps, we could find ourselves arriving at a location off the general shipping lanes whose beauty and romance could startle our indifference, impressing even the most experienced of seamen. Such a place was Tahiti.

Approaching the island we reduced speed having arrived early dawn. Scaling the bridge ladder, I was grateful that the tropical weather had seen the steering position transferred to the open air 'Monkey Island' wheelhouse, affording me a perfect view of the developing, magnificent spectacle that was to register in my memory for a lifetime.

The fading moonlight still bathed us in the last of its eerie soft cast, for off the port bow a giant silver full Moon hung low like a lantern over the nearby mysterious sister island of Moorea. An equally sized brilliant golden Sun was climbing relentlessly from behind the black tooth-like mountains of Tahiti right ahead of our bows, its heat already raising wispy curtains of vapour from the enchanting islands. Two heavenly bodies simultaneously illuminating two of Earths most beautiful treasures, so awesome the scene, I almost questioned the evidence of my vision.

With the improving light the islands were now developing into various shades of greens, gold's and purples rapidly changing with splashes of brighter coloured habitation also becoming visible. Both were now seen to be set in a crystal clear deep blue sea somehow increasing the beauty of an already breath-taking panorama. Closing the land the more pronounced became the scented breeze of a billion flowers and blossoms, enriched by the exciting dank smell of the undergrowth.

A balanced scene of marvellous beauty displayed itself now, with the sun climbing victorious over Tahiti, whilst the full moon posted over Moorea surrendered its dominance

*Around the Buoys*

gracefully as the sky completed its transformation from starry velvet to a clear azure blue. Conversation was non-existent. Each man spellbound. They realised it was one of those transient 'once in a lifetime' sights. The magnificent and almost indescribable beauty would haunt our memory lockers forever.

I secretly prayed for time to stand still, even pleaded for it to drag more slowly, reluctant to lose the magic as I drank in the wonder before me but Nature, busy with its artistic creations sadly took no heed of a simple Liverpool deck hand. If the island itself was as beautiful as the approach, we were in for a wonderful visit.

Swinging through the breakwater entrance of the picturesque lagoon type harbour of Papeete, white hulled schooners working copra at various berths, looked as if they had been purposely positioned for a pleasing effect. A cock crowed. Two attractive wahines waved. The Third mate realised, "No wonder there was bother aboard the "Bounty!" A large painted sign on the side of a warehouse read, "Iaorana deTamare Tahiti."

"Welcome to the Flower of Tahiti?" I guessed.

I didn't need to guess that my bewitching arrival was originally by the courtesy of Gravesend's Magical Passport.

*Bill Backshall*

**Memory's Locker**

Have I dreamt or did it happen, did the salt wind sting my lips?

Was that cream-like wake a fancy as I passaged lovely ships?

Shooting stars and phosphorescence perhaps a figment who can say

Did I see her shipping green seas, smile the porpoise at their play.

At evenings watch such memories bubble from the depths of bygones keep

All the wonder of the oceans from the locker anchored deep

Visions of a barren coastline, beauty of a lagoon beach.

From Northern berg to tropic isle no far flung spot denies its reach.

Distant harbours, squally rainbows, rolling sea swell, were they true?

Tell me if you've lived a tempest, known the deepest ocean blue.

Memory's locker holds such treasures when we trawl those hull down days,

Vivid colours, sun or sea mist, figments of remembered praise.

*Around the Buoys*

Then let me drift when beauty floods me, canvas me that ghostly sea

Sooner dream with sometime spirits, share their sea room wistfully'

Neither tide nor time contain me, no slave to laws captivity

A key turn in our memory's locker, bestows the gift to passage free.

**Patchwork**

My father was the most honest, loyal, sincere man I have ever known, and I write this knowing that we observe our own kin through rose tinted glasses. Along the line of the Liverpool docks, everybody had a good word for 'Old Charlie'. He was also the world's worst carpenter, evidenced by the ramshackle pigeon lofts and sheds he erected. Old second hand timber was just nailed roughly together, and even hinges were made from the leather tongues cut from cast off shoes. Everything was 'Just blaady tempory' as he threw down his hammer, for he'd been born in Bow, London and still retained his Cockney accent despite living in the 'Pool' for many a year.

One day hanging around between ships, he said to me, "Bill, my old mate Sammy is not in the best of health and wants to sell his partly converted steel lifeboat shored up on the Gladstone Dock. Why not go down and buy the thing?"

So I did just that and in doing so cemented a good friendship with Sammy the owner.

However, with him being an older, married and conscientious man, and though he never passed comment, I sensed he didn't approve of my irresponsibility, drifting between ships, quitting jobs, drinking in pubs with old shipmates, resenting authority, single man's stuff like that.

The cabin Sammy had been erecting on the boat looked dreadful something like a hen shed, with square sides and windows, and a pitched roof like a terrace house. It was so ugly I wondered whether my father had been called in as the Marine architect. So dismantling the old woodwork, I rebuilt things, a nice camber to the decks, streamlining the cabin and wheelhouse to follow the pleasing lines of the hull, raking aft any perpendicular faces, making her look quite smart. Serving a few years as an apprentice joiner before my training at Gravesend sea school, certainly helped things.

Being a 'dumb' lifeboat, provision now had to be made for a stern tube to be fitted and with no electric power available on the site, this entailed manually hack-sawing through the metal stern post. Luckily for me, a coppersmith bought a neighbouring craft and obliged by welding the tube in position. My next task was to make this job watertight by building up a large bulbous patch around the area with successive coats of fibre glass, and just on completion, a vehicle arrived heralding the old owner Sammy.

"I've come to see what sort of mess you're making of the

*Around the Buoys*

boat Bill!" he joked as we shook hands. Obviously he still retained his interest in small craft, and though he made no further comment, I could see he approved of the woodwork, etc., in progress. Then, after inspecting the impressive patch around the stern tube, he straightened up gasping rather than breathing normally for air, sadly old age as well as his poor health was catching up with him. His bright blue eyes stared at me thoughtfully for a second or two, and then he decided to trim my vents. "Bill," he said shaking his head, "Bill, you can put a patch on the stern of a boat O.K, but you'll never be a patch on your old fellah's arse!"

I got his drift all right. He rightly valued my father's honesty, loyalty and sincerity far more than my fancy carpentry.

**Gravesend Rocket**

As a young man of just eighteen, I reported to the Merchant Navy training school at Gravesend along with 18 other very green boys. Apart from the lessons, I was naturally very interested in the flying bombs (V 1s) that were flying parallel with the Thames about that time with quite a number passing directly overhead.

However, none dropped close enough to cause concern and having lived in dockside Liverpool during some very heavy raids as a youth, I was used to bombing, that is, if you could get used to the ordeal. Most of the schools complement slept in smelly air raid shelters by the sea front gardens, but a class on watch duties was detailed to sleep in the barracks building itself for security reasons.

During my classes watch all went well one night with we lads sleeping soundly, but during the early hours we were rudely awakened by a tremendous explosion. I finished up lying half out of my bunk wondering what had happened then further alarmed by the sounds of falling glass and cascading water from some storage tank overhead.

Shocked, but already sleeping partially dressed, we rushed outdoors and through the entrance gates a matter of yards away, where we came upon a dreadful sight with the houses opposite completely demolished to rubble. Already the rescue men were arriving, and in attendance, at times calling for complete silence, hoping for any trapped people to indicate where they lay by shouting for help.

Sadly, we gave what little help we could and the next morning we tried again to help the distressed people of the area salvage material from their completely wrecked homes. The scale of death and destruction reminded me of the carnage caused by powerful 'land mines' (Parachute bombs) etc. that I had experienced at home in Liverpool, absolutely horrific on simple housing communities.

*Around the Buoys*

Later in the morning at a small demolished building across the road, I watched rescue men carefully withdraw a female's body from the rubble causing a man in the crowd to break down in tears. He was comforted by his heartbroken friends. I believe it was a Maternity Clinic.

Next day, I joined some class mates manning a cutter to row three Ministry boffins out to examine an unusual object exposed by the low tide lying beyond the school waterfront on the Thames mud banks. Discussing it, the three men seemed nonplussed, but confirmed it had been blown from the bombed site right over the school premises and out into the Thames by the blast. Metal, six to eight feet long, some four to five feet in diameter with roughly two cone shapes married at the narrow ends, the whole thing was covered in a complex of wiring, pipes and other devices.

We lads couldn't make head nor tails of the thing and the scientists weren't helpful in any way. In fact, they stood detached and secretive when discussing it.

When eventually news of rocket attacks were made public, we realised it was the engine of one of the first V2 rockets that were then beginning to fall on South East England.

One day towards the end of our three month course, we watched the sky full of Dakota planes flying high over the area on a mission to the battle torn continent; carrying courageous men to land at deaths door, I realise now it was Arnhem. They brought to my mind the R.A.F's motto "Per Ardua Ad Astra", "Through Hardships to the Stars". The brave people of Gravesend suffered one of those terrible hardships that night on Mankind's journey to the stars, for that rocket, masterminded by Walter Von Braun, was the fore runner of the vehicle that ferried man to the moon and beyond...

**Cunard Cinderella**

As a wee boy, in a convoy consisting of my other brothers and sisters, we would visit my lovely old Gran's house on Sunday afternoon, and if we were very well behaved we were allowed to peep into the mysterious front room and wonder at the curios there'.

Carved wooden creatures from Africa, beautiful ornate pictures from Venice, brassware from India, plaques form Chile, etc. Then I would be enchanted by photos of the Cunard liners "Antonia" and "Laconia" hanging on the wall in my Gran's hall.

However, the "Samaria" took pride of place being my Aunt Ann's favourite liner, for she had served aboard her, as opposed to the other liners, for many a year as a stewardess. In my child's mind, though, she was second in importance only to the Captain.

Ann's cheerful nature was her passport to befriending passengers from all walks of life, and her many stories about the "Samaria" included how on certain occasions, dressed in her finery she would, against the rules, daringly slip into the

*Around the Buoys*

first class saloon, hob-nob and dance the evening away with the famous and the rich. "Only to retire back to my cabin at eight bells," she would sigh, "Just like a Cunard Cinderella."

In time, probably fired by my Aunts yarns, I was lucky enough to attend the Gravesend Sea School and after completing my deck training eventually found myself in Bombay serving aboard a Liberty type cargo ship. Ashore one evening, I surprisingly ran into three close buddies of mine who lived close to me in Liverpool and later, after celebrating, we made our way back to their vessel which I was pleased to discover was none other than the liner "Samaria", my Aunts old favourite Cunarder!

I slept aboard overnight in the stewards 'Glory hole' and in the morning when I awoke, my three pals had already 'turned to' which gave me a chance to visit where I thought my Aunt Ann would have trodden the decks, I could now discuss the liner all the better when next we met.

Having become used to smaller cargo boats, it took me an embarrassing length of time finding my way off the damned passenger liner and I felt a mug asking the deck hands how to get ashore. I swore I'd stick to tramp steamers and leave liners to the big boat men.

Years later and now on the beach, I began to visit my Aunt, now sadly aged and fragile living in a sheltered accommodation. You can be sure the "Samaria" was never far from our conversations. Sadly, upon arrival on my last visit I was told by the Warden my Aunt had just passed away, in fact Doctor Aria, a charming very caring physician of Middle East appearance was still in attendance.

Waiting patiently, my eyes fell upon an envelope on the Wardens reception desk with the Doctors full name and address upon it,"Dr Samarkand Aria", Swanpool Lane, Aughton, Lanc's. Struck by the unlikely coincidence, I knew that Ann would have cheerfully addressed him as Dr "Sam" or "Sam Aria".

The Cunard liner "Samaria" had cared for her on her passages around the World and now Dr "Sam Aria" had cared for her passage out of it.

**Suez Side**

Following my deck training at Grave end in 1944, and months into a long tramping voyage, I found myself coming off the 8-12 watch whilst serving aboard the SS "Samlister", a war time Liberty type ship, She was steaming serenely through the night time narrow Suez canal, bound for Genoa from Lourenco Marques with a cargo of coal. Earlier misfortune, though, had created a shortage of helmsmen, with only A.B.s being allowed to the wheel through the passage.

The Bosun, a war scarred eccentric to say the least, who probably hadn't steered a ship for many a long year was pressed (against his wishes) into taking the wheel for a two hour spell, relieving my watch mate at midnight. Five minutes later, just as I prepared to jump into my bunk, the

*Around the Buoys*

vessel suddenly trembled, the ship's siren began blasting five loud continual short whistles and the engine room telegraph bells rang loud and furiously. Pandemonium!!

"We haven't had the bloody hammer have we?" somebody shouted, puzzled, but in no great panic knowing the war was now thankfully over. Rushing on deck I was shocked to see our vessel was athwart the canal well aground, blocking the convoy of ships astern of us. Luckily they had heard our distress signals and were now mooring themselves safely. We then unsuccessfully attempted to warp ourselves free during the bitterly cold night, but eventually had to await a tugs arrival in the early morning to haul us free and so on to Port Said for a diver's survey.

After his inspection he reported there was 'no damage'. "Only to our pride," corrected the Mate, shaking his head ruefully, then with a wry smile he turned to the now subdued Bosun. "Hitler tried for five long years to block this canal up and failed. Yet you managed to block it up in five bloody minutes Bose!"

The Bosun, christened "Black Morgan" by the cheery Liverpool deck hands, not only for his swarthy appearance and beard, but also for his obvious conservation of toilet soap, said "The wheel got jammed!" then gave a little sort of dance, hopping from foot to the other, hunching his shoulders with both arms outstretched and, sticking his tongue out the side of his mouth, appeared to offer this performance as some sort of explanation and apology.

You could only shake your head in wonder at the spirit of this man whose body had been scarred and burnt terribly whilst escaping from a torpedoed burning tanker. Who said the Merchant Service wasn't full of characters?

**Sea Scape**

Being an aged but conscientious man, I feel duty bound to remind seafarers of this long outstanding warning. Therefore, excuse me if I take you back to a long ago war, the outbreak of which prematurely ended my elementary school education.

However, Eric Mercer my class chum and myself, upon leaving those hallowed concrete walls, were soon to receive a further but more drastic education spending nights dodging the Luftwaffe's bombs and viewing the resulting fires and damage. Living alongside the Liverpool docks in wartime wasn't an idyllic spot to spend ones youth, (or even in peacetime come to think of it).

Eventually we split company, he disappeared into the wartime confusion and off I went to Gravesend for deck hand training which really was out of the frying pan into another frying pan, getting mixed up in the then flying bomb raids and later some persons unknown dropped one of the early V 2 rockets alongside the school damn near wiping us out as it caused death and destruction around the area.

*Around the Buoys*

Luckily I managed to survive those hazards and even the early morning coffee which was just another serious wartime threat I passed the exam at the end of the three months course feeling very proud of myself, until I realised that everybody else had passed. I realised we probably would have passed with turnips instead of heads on our shoulders, deck hands being in short supply at that time.

Time rolled on as it tends to do and one day whilst at home on leave waiting for a bus to take me to the Pool for another ship, I spotted Eric's mother, Mrs Mercer, approaching me off the port bow. *'Good,'* I thought, *'I'll ask her how my old school pal Eric's getting on'* but as she closed the range I grew concerned noticing that although she wasn't exactly flying a battle ensign, she exuded an aggressive air as she frowned weighing up my denim jeans, zip up Yankee jacket and long straggly hair. "Hello! Mrs Mercer," I greeted her respectfully, "How's Eric getting on?" She failed to acknowledge my courtesy flag, but immediately opened up with her main armaments. Her first salvo landed. "Why aren't you in a khaki uniform?" she thundered, "My Eric was called up last year into the Army and your both the same age, and were in the same school class!"

"Well," I apologised meekly, taken aback, and attempting a damage limitation exercise, explained, "I'm going away to sea now," hoping she would notice my little silver badge and backwater little. But no, "Tscch!" she exploded, dismissing my defence as being valueless and then fired off her second broadside, "You should be in the forces like my Eric, at least he's doing his share fighting for his country not running off to sea. No wonder we were damn near losing the war with people like you!!"

She walked away smugly satisfied at having identified another of the wars inequalities. Left floundering, I feel it is my duty at times to alert any members of the Merchant Navy still sailing, with the following.

**Mariners Official Advice Notice.**

**In the eventuality of future hostilities, join the Army and stop 'Running away to sea', or you may get a similar broadside from a Mrs M.**

### Ringing the Changes

Afore the event of marine engines, orders for altering a vessels movements were relayed by leather lunged Officers bellowing seafaring terms, often accompanied by suggestive gesticulations to sailors on high. In time the mechanical gubbins was invented and installed, but out of sight and earshot, thus calling for improved communication that resulted in the ships telegraph.

Through a manually powered system of boxed in wire cables, chains, and pulleys, and controlled from brass standards fitted with indicating lever handles. An optional engine

## *Around the Buoys*

movement menu on circular display could be selected and transmitted from the bridge to an engine room repeater.

The lever handle would be smartly moved fore and aft in a preliminary action before settling on the chosen command. This would arouse the Engineer by activating a frighteningly loud attention bell designed to overcome the noise barrier caused by nasty pieces of heavy machinery clanging dangerously around. This telegraph system was immediate and definite and overcome earlier hazards of voice pipe and telephone signals being unheard or misheard in the general cacophony.

Eliminated also was the courteous but dangerous phone practice of tendering the Masters compliments, obligatory small talk concerning the weather, the Cooks offerings, and interesting female passengers before attention was drawn to requirements impatiently desired for urgent manoeuvres.

Upon receipt of the request, and excited by the peremptory bell, the Engineer would respond, confirming the order by answering on his own telegraph "tell-tale" reply safety device, causing the bridge telegraph to similarly ring, albeit quieter, with his pointer hopefully endorsing the chosen command, thereby often allying bridge palpitations.

The Engineer would then cleverly demonstrate his mastery over the apparently unbridled mechanical beast by turning large shiny steel wheels, important looking valves and fiddling with mysterious handles which hopefully would cause the engine, and thence the vessel to perform as desired. All in all, a simple but efficient system.

Certain large liners were additionally equipped with 'Docking Telegraphs' with their repeaters gracing the poop. They offered an optional menu of mooring commands, but suffered from an inferior relationship with the imperious Bridge/Engine room type. Sparingly used by the bridge staff, often only to check the device still functioned, or to cheer the Second Mate who, during docking activities, could be seen loafing around looking left out of things.

The Officer was compensated however by basking in the admiration of boat deck female passengers impressed by the handsome sparkling brass things, for when well-polished, the poop telegraphs looked very pretty as opposed to the untidy deck clutter of vents, derricks, mooring lines, winches and especially deck hands.

A large percentage of telegraphs were made by Chadburns Ltd and A&R Robinson Ltd in Liverpool causing them to be referred to as the "Chadburn" by many foreign seamen. Sadly, as with the "Leather Lunged" system, progress has overtaken the handsome telegraph with most of the makers having closed down or diversified into other products.

The writer lived nearby Chadbourn's workshop, was employed by their rivals Robinsons, and later assisted in the repairing and overhauling of shipboard systems by Maddox Ltd a further maritime company. That background later resulted in a comforting reassurance when seafaring after Gravesend sea training, for one could relate to the instrument makers familiar names and one often gave the telegraphs a secret nod, a friendly wink, and a deserving pat as one would do to a loyal obedient dog.

"Stand By!"

"Stop!"

"Finished With Engines."

## Cook's Adrift

I learnt a lot at the Sea School, but something I didn't need to learn, which was already in my locker, was a mistrust of authority. Born in dockside Liverpool it was accepted, especially amongst young men, that people in uniform or formal suits, were natural enemies and thumbing a nose at, or disobeying them, created a sense of cheerful satisfaction. Any additional 'fall out' inconvenience caused was a bonus.

Generally, this feeling simmered harmlessly on the back boiler, but alcohol could turn the gas up. After a farewell drink in a dockside Bootle pub delayed sailing our rusty Fort boat, we berthed in Baltimore for a fortnight, where we were refused a cash 'sub' blocking any further alcohol consumption.

Thence a passage that would last over two months to Auckland N Z. The causes of this lengthy trip was to load oil drums at a desolate long pier in the Red Sea, which we found hard to believe had Africa attached to the other end.

This mooring provided only boredom. Also, steaming at a modest 9 knots provided by some embarrassed red-faced engineers didn't exactly create a bow wave of any great proportions.

Finally arriving at N Z, meant we had been three months teetotal and looking for a possible wee glass or two. Sadly, our thirsts remained unsatisfied when our suspiciously named Captain Tough again refused an issue of cash. This resulted in ships equipment disappearing and drink magically appearing. Drunkenness followed, with its accompanying disobedience and rowdyism. Though it caused inconvenience for the bridge staff, it was simply good fun to the sailors, kicking over the traces in the time honoured, "Kiss my Stern-end," tradition.

Things soon settled down until we next arrived At Newcastle, Aussie, and even though no money was again forthcoming, alcohol was produced, albeit illegally causing further bouts of Officer head scratching.

Things once again quietened down, but the third morning there brought bewilderment to all hands, finding the galley equipment lying strewn around the main deck. Pots, pans, other and utensils scattered everywhere, but no sign of the Chief Cook nor his prickly heat rash. He'd ran afoul of an old shipmate ashore, got drunk, then spitefully thrown his gear out of the galley and then gone adrift for another drunken party ashore with the second cook in tow. There was no breakfast, creating uncertain smiles amongst the sailors.

*Around the Buoys*

Later, though, with no dinner forthcoming, scowls were now in evidence. The absence of an evening meal finally created a minor mutiny with the deck gang marching to the 'Old Man's 'deck complaining, demanding to know what the hell was going on, for though we were starving, the Chief Steward was managing to feed the midships crowd.

The Captain patiently explained, "Well men, just as you do occasionally, the Cook's kicked over the traces and thumbed his nose at authority. I suppose if it's all right for you men to perform like that now and again, surely it's all right for him to do the same?"

We were completely shocked, "Oh no! That's not fair!" We were absolutely indignant, "Hell no! It's not right when the Cook goes adrift!" But Captain Tough shrugged sympathetically, "Men, if you want to live by the sword, you've' got to expect to perish by it."

We had great difficulty digesting that profundity, but seeing that we didn't have much else to digest we finally had to swallow it.

I've always had the feeling I started to grow up during that trip.

**Selvagee Syndrome**

During out deck training at the Gravesend Sea School, our greatly admired Instructor was a West countryman, Harry

Challenor, but occasionally we were indebted for the odd lesson to a slim London Instructor we vaguely knew as "Knocker". To be honest, we didn't get the opportunity to know him very well, but enough to know that though he was a pleasant, sincere helpful man, with a forthright manner and a loud voice that was employed excessively, he held a strange fixation with Selvagee Strops.

Aboard the "Tuareg" a damaged French liner then used as our part time training ship lying mid-stream, when under his tuition we would be taken down a hatch and after discussing and exhibiting the difficulty of wire splicing, he would then shepherd us on to his favourite subject the values of the Selvagee strop, how to make one, how it originated, how to use one, in fact he covered every facet of the thing.

However his speech was rather quickly delivered in his Cockney dialect and to we slow Northerners a lot was lost in translation. This didn't deter 'Knocker' and on the next occasion he would again press home his lecture about the obscure strop, it seemed that any chance of conversation was just an invitation to publicize his 'stropfulness,' as my pal Johnny put it.

This caused it to register deeply in my mind, for I gathered the strop is made of loosed stranded ropes and seized together with spun yarn, but even today I'm a little unsure about them and frankly I've never seen, nor heard of the them being used.

## *Around the Buoys*

Duly impressed though Johnny and I joked and let our youthful imagination run wild and we wondered if a sensible conscientious A.B should ever leave home to join a vessel without one stowed deep in the old sea bag, and what a dreadful sin it would be to be caught stropless late at night in a brothel or adrift in mid Atlantic in an open boat, what excuses could you make? We humorously wondered should we meet him in the years to come what his opening subject would be.

Well the old tempus fugit's, and I became employed in seafaring life, time spent tramping, then some years in Holts of Liverpool etc., like the rest of the Gravesend men putting time and distance between ourselves and those days at the training ship. Eight years later I joined Elder Dempster's vessel the M.V. "Sekondi" loading at Tilbury for West Africa, and as we rigged the Jumbo stays from the table, I had a good view across the river and naturally focused on the old school site. I stood quietly for a spell, for of course it took me back all those years reawakening memories of my time there, the Instructors, the wartime rocket that damned near killed us all, the flame tailed V1s, the early morning sprints around the sea front gardens, the frightening morning coffee etc. Yep! I felt truly nostalgic.

Later, sitting in the mess, the Bosun told us a shore gang was aboard lashing some deck cargo, etc. Suddenly and unbelievably, out of the blue a strangely familiar Cockney voice from the distant past, I'd recently been thinking about drew near and entered the mess followed later by its owner.

What a surprise! The man was a dead ringer for our old friend, the school Instructor "Knocker". I wasn't quite 100% sure, for firstly he didn't recognise me and secondly, it was some years since I had last seen him, so uncertainty reigned. I listened as he briefly reported to the Bosun they had secured the deck cargo with wire lashings and then without any embarrassment and in an Instructors manner, he started to explain to the experienced and amused deck hands how to unreel a new coil of wire rope without getting turns in it. **Then, confirming to me beyond all doubt that I had the right man, he manoeuvred the subject on to describing, and recommending the. . . Guess What?? Yes! You're Damned Right!!**

**Gunnery Course**

I visited the very interesting Albert Dock in my home town of Liverpool recently, and one of the transformed warehouses reminded me of a rough time in we older men's lives. Sometime after my sea school training in '44 I was sent with a mixed group of 30/40 seamen from the Shipping pool in Paradise Street for a two day refresher gunnery course.

Day one took us to an R N barracks along the Mersey coast near Formby called the H M S "Queen Charlotte". Winter weather meant that the smart Royal Marine sergeant who sadly for him, had no authority over us, met a bizarrely dressed motley crew of independently minded men at the nearby train station, and made a fatal mistake of suggesting

## Around the Buoys

we march in orderly ranks, arms swinging soldier style, into the barracks simply to impress the R N people. No worse suggestion could have been made to the men, who resented the Senior Service, or any other authority come to that. They strolled into the barracks in a disorderly mob, smoking, swearing, reading newspapers, and even whistling after Wrens Officers to the suppressed fury of the staff.

The instruction was very good though, dismantling and assembling weapons, learning how to stick the shells in the right ends of the guns. Sadly a light plane dragging a drogue target only made two sweeps of a promised dozen or more, for the live gunfire by the seaman was considered to be too dangerous by the pilot who must have wondered whether somebody had painted swastikas on his wings.

After a very interesting day, upon leaving relationships had greatly improved, for the men has stowed their display of independence and irreverence back in its locker, and well meant "Cheerio's" and Wishes of Goodwill echoed around. A gold ringed Officer nodded at our departure and quietly but sincerely bade the gang "Good Luck men!" He knew that chances were, a number of them wouldn't be around come the end of the war.

On the second and final day of the course we visited the particular warehouse at the Albert Dock that had jogged my memory all these years later. Inside at that stage, the ceiling had been cleverly converted into a large dome representing the sky and after various instructive films were screened, identifying enemy planes, how to apply gun 'aim off' etc., the lights were lowered, the audio speakers turned up extra loud, and a film of an actual air raid attack on a Mediterranean convoy was focused onto the dome making it surprisingly realistic.

It appeared as though the planes were attacking the audience as if aboard a targeted ship. The falling of bombs from high level raiders, the screaming and frightening noise of attacking Junkers dive bombers, the explosions of the bombs, the continual barrage of gunfire, the smoking of burning vessels, the crashing of stricken planes made it all terribly life like. Amongst this havoc, advice was being given on how to apply certain techniques that may hopefully help us to combat these types of raiding planes.

Leaving the building the course completed, with the noise of the simulated raid still ringing in our ears, the men were in a subdued mood. Most of them had experienced just such a fireworks party and it seemed unreal somehow to be walking home quite safely and detached from that horrific filmed attack.

*'Awkward, disrespectful sods'* these men were called by some, but the same men would be cheerfully reporting to the 'Pool' on the morrow, and the next day, ready to join a ship that quite probably might terminate with a... **'Voyage Not Completed'** discharge.

*Around the Buoys*

**A N'ICE TRIP**

The banana/fruit boat "Cavina" was built with cooling arrangements naturally taking priority over heating comforts and therefore certainly wasn't the vessel for a Winter North Atlantic crossing. Even so, after normal trade runs were interrupted by hostilities, a cargo was a cargo no matter where it was chartered for, even the W.N.A, and unluckily she had been chartered for just that, a victim of the end of the war scramble to take any inducement and the newly signed crew were apprehensive knowing what would be encountered crossing to Halifax in late December.

The bitterly cold passage covered the New Year and though en route to the wheel house we deck hands glimpsed passengers and Officers celebrating sixteen bells snug and warm in the saloon, whilst in the focsul men were more concerned with trying to keep free from freezing by being continually rigged in every stitch of clothing we possessed, towels included.

Approaching Nova Scotia, the icy conditions worsened alarmingly with the vessel covered in frozen Ice and snow. Perished, I stood 'Look-out' for two hours on the monkey island at 3am, when a polar bear appeared. Luckily it turned out to be the Second Mate in his brownish cream duffle coat.

The standard compass light had failed and he invited me to hold his torch whilst he checked his readings. The two pair of gloves I wore made me fumble and drop the thing which then rolled out of sight under the decking. With my ears being pleasantly warmed by the Second Mate's observations, I groped around unsuccessfully.

Panicking, I stupidly I slipped off my right hand gloves the better to feel for the damned thing and believing I was successful, I grasped hold of, then found my hand firmly stuck to a frozen bare metal pipe. It was like an electric shock and after a struggle I simply had to tear my hand away, pulling off small slices of skin and flesh. My cries of pain and obscene curses amused the Officer who kindly returned with a bandage; however, my hand was now too frozen to bleed.

The short voyage completed, back home in Liverpool, starting to enjoy my leave, I entered our 'Music Room' so called because we had an old piano and a radio gram stuck in the gloomy front parlour. I sorted through some records awkwardly for my hand still hurt, casually selecting what to me was an unknown classical record belonging to my sister, and soon I was emotionally uplifted by the wonderful music and the magnificent vocal performance. It would register in my memory indelibly.

Desperate to know the title I struggled in the fading light to read the tiny title, finally managing to focus somewhat, finding it was a piece from Puccini's "La Boheme" sung by the Italian tenor Gigli. However, the rest was in very small print making it difficult to read in the late afternoon winters gloom, it looked like the title was in Italian something like "Che Gelida Manina" which didn't make much sense to me.

*Around the Buoys*

Impatiently borrowing the small torch from the electric fuse cupboard I promptly dropped it from my aching hand for it to roll out of sight under the cupboard. Recovering the thing I paused on all fours then sniggered out loud at the unlikely coincidence that occurred aboard the Cavina. "At least this time I won't get bloody frostbite!" I cursed gratefully.

Shining the beam on the label, I finally managed to read it all including the smaller English title translation, **it read . . . "Your Tiny Hand is Frozen."**

**"B" Flag Bang**

**SS "Malakand"**

**(T&J Brocklebank, Liverpool)**

In the month of May a newspaper article reminded me of a terrible event that occurred seventy years ago, causing me to dredge *deeply into* my memory locker to recall that as a youth, I stood outside my home in Liverpool relieved and relatively calm now that an extremely heavy air raid was over. I breathed the sickly sweet pine smell of burning timber yards, mixed with the nasty smell of burning and devastated buildings as I gazed at the dust and smoke filled angry bright red sky that reflected the enemy bombers nights work. Suddenly I was startled and nervously shocked as a tremendous deep explosion occurred coming from the dockland direction. It was not too exceptional and long lasting to have been caused by a delayed action bomb or a parachute land mine, nor was it A, A fire.

I simply couldn't grasp what could have caused such a frightening blast, especially seeing that the Luftwaffe had departed by some hours now, probably more than satisfied with their nights work. Sadly the horrific explosion signalled the destruction of the cargo vessel SS "Malakand", the surrounding Husskison No2 Dock with installations, numerous warehouses, and part of the Overhead railway system, in fact destruction of the whole area.

"Malakand" had been loaded with a thousand tons of ammunition for the Middle East war zone, but during the raid a drifting barrage balloon had somehow become entangled with her rigging and on falling to the deck had burst into flames. A shower of incendiary and exploding H E bombs added to the chaos hampering firefighting efforts.

Brave and persistent attempts by Captain Kinley, his crew, dockers and firemen failed to save her from becoming fully ablaze from stem to stern and she was eventually man handled to mid dock in an unsuccessful attempt to scuttle her.

*Around the Buoys*

Beyond saving now and creating an imminent deadly threat with her cargo, "Malakand" was finally abandoned to her fate with the area hurriedly cleared to safeguard life. Swept with flames she eventually detonated with the tremendous explosion that I can still recall all these years later, heavy metal plates and debris found three miles away.

Thankfully but still, sadly, there were only four deaths, two men who had been bravely assisting in the efforts, and a young married couple who, unfortunately, were driving past on the dockside road at the time

**Footnote:** It took a thousand tons of exploding ammunition to wipe out one dock and one ship from the face of the Earth, but modern day container-isation has created the same effect to a thousand more Docks without so much as a whimper.

**Say Can U Sea?**

A fine Sunday morning in Baltimore saw my old Gravesend shipmate Johnny C' humorously inviting me to join him by going ashore and walking across the good ole USA. That is, I suspected, until dinnertime when hunger would bring us back to the rusty, old SS "Fort Richelieu" we were serving aboard.

Starting our few thousand mile journey we were not too far down the road before we were surprised by seeing the local youths playing what they called Soccer, for we were led to believe that football wasn't very popular in the States at that time. However, the sponsored teams were well turned out with the match being well organised and they played with great enjoyment and spirit, but sadly one team named Blogg's Meat Mart conceded a number of silly goals causing Johnny to criticise the defence with a few old Liverpool Kop gee-ups. "Show some fight!!"

"Face the ball and get stuck in!" and then he shouted, "You couldn't defend against eleven old ladies."

Judging by the looks thrown our way, especially after the last remark, they weren't too well received, so we sensibly pressed on with our safari before the final whistle was blown.

We trundled deeper into the continent, well say at least half a mile coming eventually to a series of beautifully laid out lawns. "Them's well 'manured' lawns," said my pal. After some thought I realised the word he had in mind was manicured. Edged plaques described various States, when and how they joined the Union etc, and then looming before us stood an old, large stone building hard to describe, but suggesting an ancient fort or battery.

"Must be a place of National importance," we agreed, which seemed a good guess for more and more vehicles were arriving discharging what were obviously sightseers burdened with the usual cameras, cigars, popcorn and all decked out in leisure clothing. Though the National flag flew everywhere, curiously, we espied the one that flew over the

*Around the Buoys*

building carried only 15 stars, "The state of the Union at some particular time, many years ago," we wondered.

The whole area was awash with a tangible air of American pride and as we progressed to the front of the building facing the Chesapeake Bay, we spotted a pair of old world cannons pointing seawards before discovering a large plaque high on the entrance walls. Pausing, and with growing unease, we read the inscription.

Two hundred years ago this Fort McHenry lay under the guns

of the English Royal Navy anchored in the Bay, with little hope of success. A Washington lawyer sent to secure the release of a prisoner was detained and watched from afar the defence garrison get safely through the night's intense bombardment. In the morning, Francis Scott Keyes the lawyer, was delighted to see the Star Spangled Banner still flying proudly and felt inspired to write the words;

*Oh say can you see by the dawns early light*

*What so proudly we hailed at the twilights last gleaming*

*Whose broad stripes and bright stars*

*Through the perilous fight*

*O'er the ramparts we watched*

*Were so proudly streaming.*

Surrounded by an intensely patriotic flag waving crowd, we silently digested this important facet of the country's history. Then suddenly I felt an urgent tug on my jacket sleeve and Johnny C' whispered to me, "Bill! This is an old American Fort! Let's get back to our old English 'Fort' before they realise we're a couple of Limey's." I agreed and quietly recommended, "I wouldn't shout anything about being unable to defend against old ladies now if I were you."

**Under the Flag**

Occasionally, and even then only briefly, time can be a little confusing like a needle stuck on an old gramophone record. For instance, Fremantle is a busy port on the bottom left hand corner of that sizable country Australia, and one weekend aboard a cargo vessel, a few of we deck gang took a trip up the river Swan to visit the modern city of Perth where the hot sunny day and the strong Aussie lager proved a little too much for me.

Finding myself adrift from my mates, I toured the city alone; eventually arriving in Kings Park where a little befuddled I read a sign "Mount Eliza". For some unknown reason "I feel at home here," I sniggered, for they were my two Christian names. However I didn't realise the significance of that remark until much later. Unfortunately, still groggy, I tripped on the kerb and sprawled on the pavement flags finishing face up.

*Around the Buoys*

With a strange 'Deja vu' feeling becoming stronger, I lay prostrate and looking up saw the National Southern Cross flag fluttering above me. *'Must be an important civic building'* went through my head and at the same time I felt unusually comfortable lying there. Two leather skinned 'Fairdinkum' guys hauled me to my feet and after thanking them, I slowly continued my sightseeing with the names of William, George and Eliza still strongly in my mind along with that vague sense of this has happened before, or better, I've been here before.

**Liverpool, England.** Many years later. Tourists arriving from Perth bearing the same family name as myself checked our local phone directory, spotted our unusual surname and made themselves known. Eventually on meeting we found that they were indeed distant relatives. After great rejoicing, one presented me with a postcard bearing a photo of a brass inlaid pavement flag laid in front of a civic building in St George's Terrace, Perth, dated 1989. This flag bore the names William Backshall and wife Eliza who arrived with their family aboard the sailing ship "Simon Taylor" as emigrants 1842.

The story unfolded that celebrating the 150th anniversary of the city's founding, the local officials decided to commemorate the names of prominent citizens who had made their mark in life, and included a few early settlers names from the then called Swan settlement by laying flags inscribed in a main city centre street. One selected was my family forebear and namesake. The original William Backshall arrived in 1842, and his inscribed gravestone flag was laid in St Georges Terrace 1989. I myself arrived in 1945 a little over 100 years later without knowledge of this history and lay prostrate on the flagstone spot he would eventually occupy, preceding him by some14 years.

Now let me try and get this straight. He arrived before me and I came after him, O K. But I was also before him as well as being after him. That was after he was before me, of course, for I was I there before him even though he was before me, but then after me on the flagstone. I'd best go and lie down under the flag in my garden to figure this lot out.

**Canal Waves**

I learnt to swim in the Leeds and Liverpool canal. Not that local folk ever used its formal name; it was simply called the "Cut" as it meandered through our industrial neighbourhood. On summer days, sometimes with my brothers, sometimes with my school mates, and often with other local lads, we would scale the canal wall, undress on the towpath, and with those lucky enough to own a costume hurriedly slipping it on, we would dive into the dark waters whooping with delight.

The centre of attraction was a huge submerged pipe on the far bank constantly discharging pleasantly hot water from the nearby factory's boiler room. This was well known as the "Scaldy", and provided free entertainment to boys from far

*Around the Buoys*

and wide. In addition some lads would bring along bars of soap provided by their mothers, and enjoy an 'al fresco' bath, but whether they eventually arrived home any cleaner was questionable.

Others would daub their bodies in bizarre patterns with the surrounding soft red clay, and after parading around in imitation war dances of the Redskin Indians they'd seen at the local cinema matinees, by jumping back in the water they proved themselves to be still 'Pale skins'. Older lads performed recognised swimming styles, but we younger kids engaged in what was called "Doggy" so-called after watching our four legged friends struggle after accidentally falling in the water.

I learnt to dive in a fashion progressing from "Belly flops" that left my stomach red and smarting, to a slightly improved entry, ungainly but safer. At the bottom of the dive the water was inky black, and on slowly surfacing, it would change to a dark brown, then a lighter brown, finally becoming clear only a few inches from the top. What a brew! Why the swimmers never came down with a dreadful disease will never be known.

Great care needed to be taken to manoeuvre past sunken rusty prams, bike wheels, unwanted furniture, and other shipping hazards, especially when older youths bravely dived from the nearby railway bridge that crossed 12 foot high over the canal. A longed for major attraction was the sighting of a horse drawn barge. Other activities would cease as the group of lads ran along to greet, then pester the soon to be irate bargeman by boarding, and diving off his craft repeatedly.

Another trick was to place their feet on the prow and be pushed along with a number of lads joining in a similar position. Numerous other antics would provoke the 'Bargee' into throwing small pieces of coal at them from his bunker to dissuade such annoyances, but generally with negative results. Then he would scamper angrily along the side deck chasing them off with his unusual wooden boots making a strange knocking noise.

However, the boys fun palled as the barge progressed south, Liverpool bound, and with the canal water cooling they returned to their far warmer beloved "Scaldy". Diesel engine barges started to make a more regular appearance making things more difficult to board the boat, but we boys persisted refusing to be denied our pleasure.

One particular 'Bargee' impressed me, for when approaching our home waters, he would park his clay pipe through the button and peak of his cap being unable to smoke, steer and harangue us all at the same time in his strange Wigan dialect. Though he would threaten and curse, we boys knew he wasn't trying too hard to catch nor frighten us, and as the craft eventually drew slowly away, he tucked the long wooden tiller under his arm, re -lit his pipe, and with a wide smile he gave we 'pirates', as he called us, a long slow sweeping wave of "Goodbye." We lads all waved back, shouting "Ta -rah Mister!"

Many years later, with my seafaring days over, I converted a steel lifeboat, ex-M V "Hinakura" into a cabin cruiser on the Liverpool docks. After much hard labour, many trials, engine problems, etc., mostly cured and corrected by good strong foul language, I finally got it something like. My ambition to use the boat for local river fishing however, was thwarted by the progress of a containerisation programme with the dock board kindly inviting me to leave and I eventually fetched up on the Liverpool canal.

Sometime later, Sally and I moored the boat, now named "Marlin", at a quiet berth near Wigan, and sitting in the cabin we relaxed, enjoying refreshments, when suddenly the patter of feet up on deck was heard, our wee craft gave a lurch and through the side window pairs of bare legs were seen disappearing, This was followed by splashes and the sound of young voices piping up.

Stepping up into the wheelhouse I could see three boys swimming across to the far bank where their clothes lay, obviously they had used the "Marlin's" side deck as a convenient springboard. I shouted angrily at them to "Clear off and keep off my boat!!"

"Sorry Mister, we didn't know you were aboard," they

chorused, with traces of the Wigan accent I recognised from the 'Bargees' of many years ago.

Returning below to my interrupted meal, I continued to grumble about 'Young boys these days have no respect for property, etc.' Sally smiled and admonished me, "For Goodness sake, Bill, don't tell me you never swam in the canal on a summers day when you were a boy?"

"I certainly did," I confessed. "But we respected other people's property those days!" and having said that, I suddenly remembered my own youthful trespasses on the barges, and quickly took a gulp of tea to keep my face straight and fight back a guilty chuckle.

With the snack over and Sally busy in the tiny galley, I took the tiller to steer the boat away from the temporary moorings, observing at the same time the three lads were still having high jinks enjoying the lovely day. Noticing the "Marlins" departure, they ceased their activities and stood watching the boat's movements attentively. Being unable to resist a feeling of warmth at seeing their happiness I tucked the tiller under my arm. I removed my old pipe, smiled, and gave them a slow sweeping wave of "Goodbye". They waved back vigorously whilst at the same time shouting "Tarah Mister!!" and suddenly bubbling up from my memory locker, I visualised my old Bargee friend from long ago days and how history was now repeating itself. I realised, exactly like him, I myself was now another link in the long continuing chain of life. The pair of us were in a way, waving a fond symbolic "Goodbye" to our own happy, carefree days.

*Around the Buoys*

## Remote Control

Years after my deck training at Gravesend, I found myself serving aboard the smart Liverpool cargo vessel S.S "John Holt" for six voyages to the West African coast. The Master, Captain Kaye was a tall man with dark unruly hair, whose features were set in a continual stern frown which discouraged any sort of casual social pleasantries even between his own Officers and the few passengers we carried.

A very reserved and correct man, social chit-chat was not his strong point and though his imperious manner kept him apart from others, he really was very well admired and thought highly of not only by the crew, but throughout the shipping line in general. I learnt from the stewards grapevine, he didn't drink alcohol, didn't smoke, nor even curse. This, to me, an easily led young scallywag was unbelievable, but his lifestyle was to eventually become an example for me to achieve. Also, he was a stickler for upholding standards, especially in the saloon where, even in the desperate heat on the African coast, formal dress was 'de rigueur'. Not a button was to be left undone otherwise his frowned look suggested you dine elsewhere. Altogether a very remote, unapproachable, straight laced Master. Still, for all that a thorough gentleman, admired for his fairness and seamanship.

Docking at London after my sixth trip we were surprised to awake the next morning to find the ship covered inches deep in snow, a complete change from the tropical weather we sunburnt sailors were used to. Finishing my midday meal I started to trudge along the snowy foredeck making my way to the focsul quarters. Suddenly I was hit by a salvo of snowballs from the bridge and I raced to take cover at the mast house ready to retaliate at the thrower, probably I assumed, one of my deck mates or one of the catering men. Looking up, to my amazement I realised it was our usually stern Captain who was the culprit. He continued his bombardment from the advantaged position of his own deck with a huge grin on his face shouting, "How about that one Backy?" referring to one good shot that hit me on the ear hole...

My reply snowballs missed by a mile, and rubbing his frozen fingers and with a waved fist of triumph he retired to his quarters, obviously well satisfied with his marksmanship. I sat in the focsul covered in melting snow, wondering if I had been dreaming or had it really happened? The aloof 'Old Man' chucking snowballs at a lowly deck hand? Unbelievable!!

Next morning the Bosun's cry was "Man to the wheel!" for we were now bound for the Mersey, and as I entered the wheelhouse the Captain stood waiting impatiently, facially as impassive as a carved Redskin Chief on a totem pole. Without turning his head, he berated me gruffly, "Come along man! Hurry up and check the wheel."

I was back to being some scruffy young Liverpool deck hand and he was just some guy with four gold rings on his sleeve as far as I was concerned. We both knew our station. The chink in his armour was well sealed up again, and his momentary lapse of returning to his happy boyhood was back under control, stowed in his memories locker for many another long year.

Later with the vessel under way ploughing the Thames past Gravesend, I peeped out of the wheel house window at the site of the sea school that was in my own happy memory locker, and then I overheard the 'Old Man' having a few strong words with the Third Mate about some minor oversight or other. As the young Officer walked out of the chartroom his eyes went to the deck head, then to meet mine and with a head shaking grin he mouthed "Miserable old so-in-so". I wasn't as convinced as I used to be.

**Personal Scuttling Log**

<u>1938</u>   As a boy I admired two impressive visiting French battleships "Strasburg" & "Dunkerque", lying at L/pool's Gladstone dock. Both were scuttled eventually to avoid enemy usage.

<u>1939</u> I stood in despair, watching from the same dock various small vessels steaming to unsuccessfully aid the stricken Sub "Thetis"' Faulty torpedo tubes accidently scuttling her in the Liverpool Bay.

<u>1939</u> I learnt with surprise the "Admiral Graf Spee" was scuttled off the River Plate to avoid further battle engagement.

<u>1941</u> A tremendous explosion I heard signalled the failed attempt to scuttle the fire swept SS "Malakand" loaded with ammunition. Husskison dock L/Pool.

<u>1945</u> I gazed in puzzlement at the abandoned partly converted Italian aircraft carrier "Aquila" moored at a quay in Genoa, Italy. Scuttled to avoid enemy usage

<u>1962</u> S S "Samlister". Once my home for near 18 months was scuttled off Halifax after earlier running aground. C. T. L. What a sad end for any vessel

**The "Black Gang"**

"What's **them** men doin' down there Dad?"

We were stood in what he called the 'fiddly', an unpleasant, dirty, smoky, steel grated, gloomy place with a hot up-rush draught. A place where I didn't want to remain too long. All I could vaguely see below, were what appeared to be two dirty clothed men shovelling or messing around in the dark between pipes and boilers and a fire thing. As they glanced up, their eyes and teeth, emphasised by the grime on their faces, gleamed like a cats, and in my child's mind, peering through the grating bars, I thought they looked like creatures trapped in a steel cage. Which, in a way, I suppose they were.

*Around the Buoys*

Occasionally on Sunday mornings Father would take a couple of his numerous children on a trip aboard the old coal fired ferry across the Mersey explaining the use of certain parts of the vessel during the passage. "They're the 'Black Gang' Son," he laughed, "but 'Marine Firemen' is their proper name. They feed and stoke the fires up to produce steam that turns the engines over".

*'I don't fancy that job when I grow up,'* I thought, and turned my back on them and their dusty grimy world as if they didn't exist. Just like the rest of society always has done.

If, in the last century, by some unusual oversight your parents failed to have you educated at Eton, Harrow, or somewhere similar, and should you have lived in a large port's dockland area, chances are you would finish up in an elementary school in one of the local mean streets. Here your fight for life's survival would begin, preparing you for employment in the nasty outside world.

Choice of pleasant work conditions after leaving school at fourteen would be very limited, but later, by a stroke of doubtful fortune, a seafaring relative or neighbour might have been misguided enough to find you employment as a Marine Fireman/Trimmer.

Imagination would indeed be sorely stretched to call it a sinecure, and in reality it could be only described as the most extremely arduous, dangerous, filthy, and unhealthy of jobs possible. Signing on as such a rating, and preparing to join a coal burning tramp vessel, did not present any great sartorial packing problems, old vests, second hand pants, shirts, any well-worn boots, shoes would do, but plenty of good quality sweat-rags should be included, their importance would become obvious as soon as the trip developed.

In harbour whilst the ships bunkers were being loaded, a Trimmers job was to attend to the side pockets making sure the coal is free running to the stokehold. Once clear of port, mainly aboard a cargo steamer, his next task would be to wind up and discharge overboard bags of ash, clinker, etc., mainly stashed and saved ready for disposal from the end of the previous voyage Then, under way, his main task is to barrow the coal from the bunker side pockets to the fireman's position, always keeping the reserve coal well stocked up.

The Fireman's job is to continually feed the voracious fires, maintaining the boiler pressure up to the watchful Engineers standard requirements. In large vessels a fireman's sole task is to fire the many boilers , but in smaller ships he may be required to "fire and trim his own", this means taking over a trimmers barrowing work in addition to his own labours. After transporting the fuel to the metal plating deck alongside the fire, he stokes up by twisting, fling-shovelling, and spreading the coal <u>evenly</u> across the fire, this ensures he loads the extreme sides and corners, preventing what was called an "Old Man", This occurs when the fuel is thrown continuously and foolishly into the centre of the fire. A practice that can cause the middle fire bars to eventually break, causing major steaming problems The often used

*Around the Buoys*

Liverpool expression "His Bars are Down!" means a person has problems through his own stupidity, originated from that situation.

With a long metal slice and rake he would also be required to be continually breaking and removing the clinker and ash away from the fire and ash pit, thus keeping the draught blowing clear through the fire bars. The waste materials when cooled were shovelled into stout canvas ash bags and dumped when the vessel was deep sea.

Older vessels had very tall funnels which provided a natural up draught keeping the fires well supplied with oxygen to burn the fuel brightly. But progress prevails, and natural draught was superseded by a more satisfactory forced draught system. These very strenuous tasks required men of experienced ability, able to pace their physical resources to last for their arduous four hour watch.

The fires are voracious for fuel and demand continual attention, giving the fireman little rest, if any, between transporting the fuel and feeding the hungry beasts, however, certain other hazards complicate these arduous tasks. The process guaranteed to have the firemen uttering continual swear words and curses is when the ship is enduring very heavy weather pitching and rolling for days on end.

At times this instability can cause the men during these trying activities, to be thrown, lurching, against very hot metal surfaces and being lightly dressed, severe burns and other injuries often occur. Of course, these accidents cannot be allowed to interfere with the Engineers steam pressure requirements.

The heat of the fires obviously create high temperatures, and those, plus the physical efforts in the stokehold combine, but still allow it to be acceptable during northern passages. However, when the vessel's destination requires passages through, as per example, the Red Sea or any such tropical hot zones, the naturally hot outside temperatures plus the fire heat itself and physical labour can become absolutely overwhelming.

Desperate firemen would be seen attempting to trim the boiler-room deck-vents, to catch even the slightest breeze, often in vain. It can be understood now why most of the "Black Gang" are generally thin scraggy types of men by coupling the extremely hard work with the conditions they need to labour under. Sweat rags as we mentioned earlier, are obviously an important piece of equipment in attempts to keep the eyes free from heavy perspiration.

The job was always filthy, and coupling this with physical exhaustion would mean the men often collapsed onto their bunks at the end of their watch falling asleep immediately. This became known as "Turning in on the Rake". "Not very hygienic," a land lubber might snobbishly remark, but a different outlook would be theirs should they try to experience the job.

During hostilities this already extremely testing job then

*Around the Buoys*

became exceptionally dangerous, for should a torpedo, shell or bomb strike the vessel a Firemen/trimmers chance of survival would be very slim, if at all. It doesn't take much imagination to envisage the scene of a torpedo's explosion near the red hot fires and scalding water in the boilers. Even with the luckiest of escapes, whilst trying to find their way up on deck, little time would be available to grab life jackets and extra clothing to survive possible outboard dreadful conditions. For weeks on end, minute by minute, any second could bring imminent disaster, but with great fortitude these men carried on regardless. Living aft on such a coal burning cargo vessel does not make for the most pleasant of voyages. As the fireman busily stokes up the thick black smoke from the stack, often blows right aft, and especially when 'Blowing tubes' continually carries with it small particles of unburnt coal, grit, ash, etc., resulting in 'red eye syndrome', soot speckled deck hands and fellow firemen, and nasty unhealthy coughing. Crew members initially attempting to wear clean white shirts etc off watch were soon likely to discontinue the practice. Occasionally the metal meal kit lids were missing or non-existent, allowing the food being carried from the midship's galley to the crews quarters aft being contaminated with a fine 'seasoning' of soot , as it was referred to. The food offered in those far off days, without being too critical, would not have satisfied an epicurean, but was generally basic according to Board of Trade recommendations, safeguarding the men from unhealthy obesity.

Sadly, being known as a "Marine Fireman" did not grant

immediate warmth nor fellowship amongst most shore folk, for their drinking habits ashore led to troublesome behaviour. Mainly pub fighting and domestic argument, which in a peculiar way, gave these men relaxation after the traumas of their seafaring life.

Through their vexatious emotions, these men were often vilified in the press and society, but these problems aside, they continually carried out the most demanding, hazardous and arduous of tasks imaginable in terrible conditions, for little reward in war and peacetime.

Despite their troublesome reputation, even to this day.

**"We Owe Them!"**

**In Stitches**

Arriving at Melbourne and hurrying to have a run ashore I showered, and barefooted with just a towel around my midships I accidentally slipped, falling down the companionway ladder. I finished up with my legs astride the bottom stanchion having bruised my thighs and slightly lacerated my scrotum. (The Chief Mate's 'medical bible's' description).

The Captain, displaying his well-known compassion for his beloved deck hands, comforted me by snarling "Good! That's bloody well stopped you from messing around ashore!"

## Around the Buoys

The Melbourne Royal Hospital's Doctor kindly invited two dozen cheerful student spectators, male and female, to watch my equipment being stitched. I'm pretty sure they enjoyed the performance more than I did judging by the broad smiles on their faces I was then issued with a pink card bearing the letters B. S. (British Seaman) which empowered me at a later appointment, to leapfrog the queues and get immediate attention, which didn't seem to please the stricken population of that city.

During the next visit, after a brief examination the Doc' seemed very interested in, and questioned me about my seafaring experiences, bad weather, tramp ships, places visited etc. He then followed this up by asking 'Had I been around the world?' and then with a curious smile he added, "Do you think it really is round?"

"Yes", I replied to the first question, "a few times". But I was in some doubt about the second query. Handicapped by an elementary education, a war luckily forced me to end over taxing my child's brain at the age of thirteen, I confessed that 'all I'd ever seen on the way around was a lot of watery stuff with bits of land stuck in the way, here and there, but as far as I knew, we never came close to falling off anywhere or anything silly like that. My shipmates later insisted he was pulling my bruised leg and the Second Mate, who I knew had a lot of clever charts and things, convinced me they were right.

Our ship moved to Geelong up the bay, and I was advised through the agents efforts, to attend a small clinic there for a final exam.' The appointment card read, "A.B. Backshall - 2:30pm". Arriving there I sat in a waiting room which I noted was populated by about thirty ladies, myself being the only male present. Most of them kept staring quizzically and even giggling at me, till suddenly, to my consternation, I realised they were all in an obvious state of advanced pregnancy. One by one, a dozen or more heavily burdened women's names were called and invited to make their rather ungainly progress through a door marked "Mr. Giles. Obstetrician" I didn't know what it meant, but I joked to myself that it sounded like the name of a T&J Harrison cargo boat from Liverpool, 'cos they all ended in the same 'ian'. After a while the nurse studied her list and called out rather hesitantly, Mrs Abbie Backshall?"

All eyes swung towards me as I blushed and, to make matters worse, I stumbled heavily to the damned door. I wished I was going to join a bloody Harrison boat.

Mr Giles coughed nervously and repeatedly to cover his shock as I made my entrance, and with a forced smile then said "Come in Abbie". After explaining that my fall was the reason for my visit, he better composed herself and after a cursory look he declared the healing process to be satisfactory. Discharging me he winked and delivered what he probably thought was a side splitting wisecrack

"I thought we were about to ring the press to hold the, front page headlines!"

Exiting the consulting room, still embarrassed by the mix up.

*Around the Buoys*

I again became the focus of curious female eyes. One cheerful mum-to-be tugged my coat sleeve and asked mischievously,

"Which did you plan for Abbie? A boy or a girl?"

"Neither," I snapped, annoyed, and, desperately wanting to clear the air by describing my fall, I explained, "It wasn't planned, it was an accident. Had I been properly dressed, I wouldn't have slipped up, and then again if I'd kept legs together I wouldn't be here today."

She burst into a fit of giggles, finally blurting out, "And so say all of us!"

I don't know what they all found so damned funny, but everyone joined in the laughter so heartily, I feared some of them were going to deliver there and then. I'll never understand women...

**Screw U**

From our dear old freighter, still a drab wartime grey and further embarrassed with red lead patches, we admired the smartly painted American vessel in her peacetime livery colours berthing across the dock. Light ship, her prop had been busily employed threshing around as the young, ever so confident Captain gave her kicks ahead and astern, for knowing he was closely observed, he determined to make a seaman-like 'one bell' mooring.

*Bill Backshall*

When safely berthed, our entertainment was prolonged when her deck hands mustered aft and lowered to the waterline, guarding the prop, two long white boards with red chevrons painted every half metre or so. Attached signs in English, Spanish and Arabic warned of "Danger!" with spaced red flashing lights setting the whole thing off.

We sighed in admiration. "When we're light ship couldn't we have a rig like that, Chief?" someone suggested to the Mate. He sighed and bravely stifling his emotions sadly shook his head. "I'd love something smart like that men, but they would look incongruous on a rusty old tramp like ours."

We certainly didn't want to look incongruous, whatever that was, but we got his drift, consoling him, "Never mind Chief, we don't want to copycat that 'Swanky Yankee!' anyway." But the precaution was sensible, for it is a dangerous area especially light ship, as was sadly underlined back home in Liverpool some years ago, when a vessel was berthing at night time in squally weather.

A gig-boat taking aboard her after mooring line, was blown under the counter by a sudden squall just as the prop threshed into action. Sadly the two men were killed and the gig-boat destroyed. Another tail end accident, this time a little more light hearted, occurred at a Blue Star boat, when Joe McRae a shore gang man, was dispatched to paint the after end draught numerals. The Shore Bosun borrowed a new alloy ladder to assist Joe reach the top numbers from the painter's scow, and he warned Joe to take every care with it.

*Around the Buoys*

Stowed aboard the scow for convenience and safe keeping was the shore gang's important tea box containing provisions, snacks, cups, etc. Also aboard, was a painter's half full drum of unused boot topping paint. All went well until suddenly the propeller started to turn, admittedly very slowly but powerfully, chopping the scow in two and throwing everything into the water including Joe.

Excited quayside spectators now shouted their own biased advice to Joe as he struck out for the safety of the rudder. The Bosun ordered him to, "Save the new ladder and disregard everything else!" A Dock Board Inspector attempted to overrule this suggestion with a cry of "Don't let that paint drum sink and pollute the dock, keep the thing safe!" whilst Joe's shore gang mates encouraged him with loud cries of "The hell with the bloody ladder and paint Joe, save our tea box!" This conflicting advice placed Joe in a dilemma, for nobody seemed concerned about his own personal welfare. But thoughts of future employment in the casual shore gang won, and to the fury of his mates and the Inspector, he grabbed the new ladder and holding it firmly, sat on the rudder watching the tea box, paint drum, etc., sink slowly.

Legal action threats from the Dock Board official echoed across the dock, and light hearted abuse and obscene language rained down upon him from his mates calling him a "F****** company's man." But seeing the shore Bosun's wink and thumbs up sign, he held on tightly to the ladder knowing he was now a registered Bosun's Blue Eye, guaranteeing preference in future employment selection.

Later, Joe's calm, sensible attitude and quiet advisory words in the engine room, directed the guilty foreman fitter to a nearby dental surgery for attention to the front loosened teeth he incurred during Joe's initial remonstrations.

**Enemy Fire**

Sometimes a child's pastime can be instructive about the harsh realities of Life. For instance, as a boy I was absolutely enraptured with the awe inspiring names of Royal Navy warships, "Resolution", "Valiant", "Renown", "Warspite", "Daring" etc, coupled with the beauty of their flowing lines and the power of their armaments. This fascination turned into a hobby for me, carving simple wooden models of these warships which eventually concentrated on H.M.S. "Glorious", an early aircraft carrier.

The reason I selected this vessel was that Rueben Winters, a young orphan, was taken in by my Mother for a little company and spoiling amongst the rest of her large family. Later he joined the R N as boy entrant to put purpose into his life. After returning home in his dashing sailor's uniform he joined the crew of H M.S. "Glorious", thus creating my personal interest in the vessel. Shortly afterwards, with the outbreak of WW2, on the home front house holders were advised, amongst many other precautions, to clear combustibles from attics, roof spaces etc., to prevent fire risks from incendiary bombs.

With this in mind, junk from our two attics including my boy's model of the "Glorious" was transferred to our garden based wooden garage. As the war progressed, during one heavy air raid the Luftwaffe dropped a tremendous amount of these incendiary bombs. Whilst successfully extinguishing those that fell within our premises, sadly one hit the garage and destroyed everything including my "Glorious" model.

Far more importantly and tragically the carrier herself sadly ran afoul of the enemy battleships "<u>Scharnhorst" and Gneisaneau</u>" off the Norwegian coast and was sunk along with her two escorting destroyers "Ardent" and "Acasta" by an overwhelming bombardment. This caused a tremendous loss of life, roughly 1,300 men perished, including my pal Rueben, barely 18 years of age. Only 30 odd men survived, rescued from a life raft by a Norwegian trawler. A great number of the crew were killed by the bombardment and the rest died in the terrible freezing conditions in the sea.

Both the "Glorious" herself and my simple boy's model of her were destroyed by enemy fire roughly at the same time. A heart breaking coincidence, that taught me a lesson about the madness of war. For I realised that the beauty and power of warships, had blinded me to the real reason for their being, which was, of course, to destroy other vessels, committing to a terrible death and shocking injuries thousands of sailors of all nationalities.

*Bill Backshall*

**CanadianDry**

Agreed his name sounded like some phoney Hollywood hero, but nevertheless, "Johnny Gallant" it sure was. Not that he cared, he just rolled along in his laid back Canadian style, popular with all hands aboard, chances are he was probably as popular on every vessel he'd ever signed on.

Generally a seaman joining a long serving tramp ship's crew keeps his head down, hoping to slowly gain acceptance, but not with Johnny. He was home and dry in the popularity stakes from the moment he placed his sized tens on the Board of Trade, such was the strength of his sunny personality.

Everybody's buddy without even trying, and the best of it was, he modestly didn't realise he was accepted so completely. A tall, slim quietly spoken guy, always with a pleasant demeanour he'd signed on in Geelong as a fireman/greaser. God knows how he'd fetched up there on the beach, probably adrift from some tramp steamer such as our own. Anyway, it felt like he'd been a shipmate of ours since the Liver Birds disappeared over the arse end fifteen months ago.

So O.K, like quite a few seafarers he enjoyed the company of 'John Barleycorn', at times somewhat a little overly to be honest. However, the whisky didn't alter his relaxed manner, drunk or sober, he maintained that cheerful charm. After a run ashore when rolling heavily back aboard, a shipmate teased him in a jocular *fashion,* "Take more water with it Johnny!" causing his smile to broaden, if that was possible. That casual remark stuck and became his shipboard sobriquet, everybody greeting or referring to him, used the same handle, "Take more water with it Johnny!"

His drinking became unshackled when we called into Papeete the port of Tahiti with a thousand tons of general, amongst which was a tempting shipment of Scotch whisky. Such bait to a sticky fingered tramp ship's crew presented an irresistible challenge which was cheerfully accepted by broaching quite a few cases. This was probably aided by the fact that the extended voyage was making the usually keen Officers a little casual about security.

Tahiti is a beautiful South Sea Island, guaranteed to lower resistance to civilisations artificial laws, making them seem vaguely irrelevant and this conscience free holiday was further encouraged by visiting friendly wahine's boarding the vessel and turning life into a pleasant whisky fuelled dream, drifting towards a modern day "Bounty" parallel, *"Take more water with it,"* revelled in the free supply of illicit shipboard whisky and the atmosphere it created, then later, realising it was Bastille Day a public holiday, and already well primed with his favourite drink, he ventured ashore to join the celebrations in the quayside taverns.

Next morning a body was seen floating alongside the vessel in the harbour lagoon and sadly it was identified as our favourite Canadian. Sailing was delayed until we gave him a decent burial, for fortunately a prosperous French passenger owned a small private cemetery and we performed the honours there. Should your vessel berth in Papeete, some ways past the Paul Gauguin museum, a small private cemetery is where Johnny Gallant lies. Roll his name on your tongue carefully, and I'm sure like myself, you'll swallow any smart arsed cracks about him, such as, 'He finally took more water with it'. He was far too admired as a man for any cheap shots like that.

**'Finito! Benito.'**

With our deep tanks full of vino and other cheap plonk we half shot deck hands boarded a tram in the centre of Genoa and commandeered the upper deck. We were bound for the dock where our vessel lay discharging, and as the tram lurched and swayed violently at various places, someone remarked," Nearly as rough as our own 28 tram ride back home in the 'Pool.

Anyway, we'd had a great night ashore and now for a good old sing-song en route, starting with 'Maggie May' and progressing to other seafaring favourites. However, shortly after getting warmed up the conductor soon tried to spoil things by poking his head up the stairs and shouting something in Italian 'Finito' or something along those lines. "Who the hell's he to try and stop our musical efforts?" we questioned. He was told to push off in choice nautical terms. "And Finito to you Benito." Our style of singing wasn't going down to well in the land of Grand Opera we reasoned. "They just don't appreciate good harmony" somebody offered and disregarding any criticism we continued with our drunken renditions.

After a short spell the guard again poked his head up the stairway yelling and gesticulating urgently. Once more he was on the receiving end of our ill-mannered refusal to stop our chorus, and advised to go elsewhere. Again he submerged down the stairs, "Stuff him," was the general advice as we started to murder that lovely song, "Yew always hert the one yew luv!"

Five minutes later, however, somebody noticed that the rocking, lurching motion had been stopped for some time now, so we put the singsong on hold and waited patiently for the tram to start again. But it didn't. After a worrisome spell with the lights going out, we traipsed enquiringly down stairs wondering what the holdup was and ready to complain about it, only to find our tram was parked in a large terminus shed surrounded by many more darkened, deserted trams with not a soul in sight.

Embarrassed and subdued, we quietly tiptoed out into the night and made the rest of the way back to our vessel on foot, realising the Guard had been patiently trying to warn us that the tram had reached the end of its evenings run. We smart guys never ever mentioned the episode between ourselves or aboard, pretending it didn't happen. But I don't doubt that with Benito it raised many a good Italian laugh at our expense when drinking with his friends.

*Bill Backshall*

**Smelling Salts**

When haunted by smells, my memory dwells on those long ago days spent at sea

Hold hard and I'll try and think of a few, let's see if you're inclined to agree.

Once clear of the quay and sailing deep sea, first you notice the clean smell of brine

Especially more, since broke on the shore, you were in a great hurry to sign.

I remember the waft of the hot oily air, belching out from the engine room door

Mixed with the soup and vegetable whiff, as the Cook stirred the stock-pot once more.

And that strong curry reek from the galley would seek, to linger in my memory

Living aft wasn't oke' when the stack starts to smoke with fumes to a nauseas degree.

Morning coffee breathed great after breakfast at eight served hot from the 'wingers tray Beats the unusual taint of boot topping paint a reminder of graving dock days

## Around the Buoys

The forecastle sports a variety of snorts, wet oilskins, and nicotine breath

It smelt pretty grim till the 'Old Man' looked in, prompting things to get polished to death

Livestock on the deck, was no joke, by Heck! The droppings would hum quite a shocker

And for many years long, it remains just as strong, in this deck hands deep memory locker

The anchor-chain mud smelt not very good, washed down with the hose as it weighs

And from hatch vents me-thinks, a variety of stinks, included nitrate and Canadian maize

Plus wet logs that reek, from the Forcados creek, and latex from the rubber Malays

Even dreamin' asleep I can still register deep, those bunkering-oil smelling days

How noses would twitch, (for this job's a bitch), when fish-oiling runners and stays

A job that smelt worse which made us all curse when done on hot tropic days.

Vile smelling potions would encourage our motion's, prescribed from the medicine box. Recommended for gout, or if you'd sadly touched out, for a dose of the crabs or for pox.

But there's one great aroma, deserves my diploma, a heaven 'scent' winner by far.

I'm addicted like hell, to my favourite smell, the nostalgic **"Stockholm'm'm Tar."**

**Paint Proud**

As a youth, I commenced serving my time to be an apprentice Joiner but being employed by a small contractors firm meant I was often required to work with the jobbers, and also an old painter who certainly encouraged me to learn the finer points of his trade. However, my training was interrupted by WW2 and at eighteen, I reported to the Gravesend Sea School and thence to the shipping world as a deck hand.

On most trips, normally the first two or three days out of Liverpool we deck hands would turn-to early mornings dressed in our heavy weather gear against the usual rain and cold winds etc., but suddenly one morning to our joy the weather would suddenly become perfect. Blue skies, strong sunshine, warm breezes, and off would come the woollies and we would single down to shorts and brothel creepers, etc., to enjoy the 'Flying-fish-weather.'

## Around the Buoys

Aboard one of my earlier vessels, we sailors were enjoying the sudden great conditions whilst painting the face of the bridge when the Bosun leaned over the rail and good humouredly addressed me. "Don't leave any holidays 'Son!" Rather proudly, but foolishly as I realised later, I boasted "Don't worry Bose', I did a bit of painting in my days ashore!" I was immediately withdrawn from the stage and lost the company of my mates as the Bosun whisked me away to paint the chartroom.

Initially I thought I was someone special being selected to carry out this important job, but what an awkward task it turned out to be. Full of intricate wiring, cables, valuable charts and delicate instruments, etc., this was no easy number and it took me a few days to finish it. Then I was spirited away to Captain's deck to paint the entire fleet of bulkheads again solo handed. I began to get a little bit disheartened and envious of my shipmates who were by now getting plenty of 'Bronzy' working on deck laughing and joking in the tropical sun.

As the weeks rolled on I was found further employment inboard painting Officers cabins, etc. and by now my deck mates were quite tanned looking the picture of health, but I was pasty faced and as white as the Cook, quite often mistaken for a member of the catering department. By the end of the four months voyage, apart from my wheel and night time look out duties, I spent most of my time painting the dammed vessels insides.

The next ship I joined I spread the word around pretty quickly that with my pasty face; I'd previously been employed ashore in an undertakers crematorium.

**Ashmosphere**

After admiring the restfully green painted Cunard Liner 'Caronia' in the Gladstone Dock, I called in a nearby canteen for a cup of hot water (said to contain tea leaves) and a tab-nab, and it was there I spotted an old pal of mine 'Griffo', a brush hand ships painter. His 'A D R' indicated he was in a serious bad mood, but hold hard, I should of course bring you up to speed about 'Griffo'.

He was a serious chain smoker with one cigarette after another wedged between his lips, and to avoid the hassle of continually removing them to finger tap the annoying ash off, he employed his own labour saving technique that discharged the ash into the immediate atmosphere. Every ten seconds or so with the 'ciggie' in situ, he would give a short but explosive puff, or two, or three to dislodge the offending deposit, but when under stress or excited, the rate would increase accordingly.

Among his buddies this became known light heartedly, as his A D R, (Ash Disposal Rate) which could be used as an assessment for influencing one's decision of whether to or not to join him in close conversation. For during a tete-a-tete his unfortunate companion would soon find themselves

*Around the Buoys*

being gradually covered in a layer of fine ash, reminiscent of a bad day at Pompeii, or of unwisely picnicking on the slopes of an active Mt Etna.

Spotting him I enquired, "How-ya blowing' it Griffo?" and then sitting opposite him, I realised I was in for an ash fall-out bordering on force seven. His speech through years of experience was now wisely delivered between the increased rate of drawing and puffing on his cigarette. "Pissed off Bill!!" he exploded cleverly utilising the first letter to blow my introductory ash cloud baptism.

"I've been working on the Cunarder and yesterday I was selected to paint the tripod mast by the foreman, and though I didn't fancy it, I finally got my part completed. This morning I expected to get some handy boat deck fleets to paint as a reward." Pausing for dramatic effect, he then changed to a fresh cigarette with a disciplined speed that would have won admiration from a Formula one pit stop team. He then continued, "But instead the foreman grabbed me and told me I'd been mistakenly been given the wrong shade of mast green paint yesterday, and then he thrust another can with the right shade at me with orders to 'Get up there and start painting the thing again!'

Well, I suggested in colourful mariner's terms, he could depart hence whist depositing his paint pot and brush up an unlikely physical receptacle! So now here I am ashore with my bladders. (Unemployment cards).

"Well, what now?" I questioned, whilst at the same time slyly activating my disengaging gear, for already an ever increasing layer of 'Griffo's' fine ash was settling on my tea cup, half eaten tab nab, jacket sleeves, eyebrows etc.

"No problem Bill," he replied. "I'm fed up with painting ships chimleys, Sampson posts, derricks etc., so I'm going after a job at Cammel Lairds over the river, where they're building two submarines. At least subs don't have stupid things like bloody masts and things sticking up everywhere!"

**Lights are Bright!**

My Father used to caution we kids, "We are born with two ears and one mouth," and though we'd query the meaning, he'd never enlarge upon the subject, knowing we'd find out soon enough later in Life.

Joining the SS "John Holt", I already knew that the vessels of that company were kept in exceptionally spotless condition, enough in fact, to make the crews of some ocean liners green with envy. This was helped on the ships arrival at the West Coast of Africa by forty or so local labour 'Kroo boys' who took over a good deal of working the ship, leaving we deck hands to concentrate on overhauling, maintenance, and painting the vessel.

The Boat Deck especially was pristine with the boats, bulkheads, rails, deckheads etc., a brilliant white enhanced

## Around the Buoys

by the scrubbed wooden near milky white deck. A nice feature at each four corners of the deck was a large metal ornate lamp and these were painted a nice restful green adding just a wee splash of colour, relieving the white and brightening things up. I'm sure people would have happily paid to simply walk around enjoying the experience.

After a couple of years serving aboard the "John Holt", I joined the "Robert L. Holt" a sister ship. Same build of vessel, same run, same everything, just a different name, really, and down the West Coast it was the usual routine Kroo Boys working the cargo, whilst we the deck crowd were busy overhauling the gear, painting etc.

Came the time to repaint the boat deck and as we got busy with the paint brushes, without thought, I quite casually mentioned to the Bosun' that, "Aboard the "John", my old ship, the boat deck lamps were not painted white like these ones, but a nice shade of restful green, and they looked great." He was really pleased with my suggestion. "Good idea Bill," he said and gave us orders to paint over the four white lamps with my suggested green. When finished, all hands thought they looked fine and I basked in the fact it was my idea.

However, the next morning the Bosun had metamorphosed into a raging madman, for he stormed into the focsul and selecting me with a sausage finger bawled,

"You ******!! In future keep that big mouth of yours shut," he snarled, "Or I'll shut it for you!"

Calming down a little he then told me the Mate had gone berserk finding the lamps painted green and had berated the Bosun sarcastically adding, "I'm bloody surprised you haven't painted the port ones red!" He then threatened to 'De-Bosunise' him if he didn't get them painted back to normal, and sharpishly too. Which I quickly and sheepishly carried out.

Luckily I was invited back the next trip because I'd now clocked on to my father's advice and guidance, 'Two ears and one tongue, Listen twice as much as what you spout.'

**Torch Bearer**

In the early days of that long ago WW2, as a young apprentice joiner I accompanied an engineer servicing the telegraphs aboard an Ellerman Lines ship, the "City of Bradford" lying in the Queens Dock Liverpool. After completing the bridge to engine room system overhaul, we turned next to the poop docking telegraphs, the casings of which ran through the Lascar crews quarters. My work entailed dismantling certain wooden panels, allowing the engineer to inspect the hidden pulleys, check the wire tensions, etc., and during these tasks, a very elderly lascar thrust a small bright blue cheap torch into my hands and pointing to the battery made it obvious he wanted me to buy a replacement for him.

*Around the Buoys*

However, at that time of shortages, No8 batteries were impossible to acquire and I attempted to advise him of this, passing the torch back. But to no avail, he was determined that I should try, and insisted on returning the thing back to me. Next I tried to indicate to him I would only be aboard for another day and therefore be unable to return with it, but sadly our communication was down to zero and in the end I surrendered to his insistence and accepted the torch wondering what I should do, for I knew that even if I was successful I still wouldn't have the time to return before he sailed. Though I tried for some days, it proved impossible to buy a new battery as I knew it would do, and as the ship lay quite a distance from my home, by the time I returned to her berth with the still unusable torch, she had well and truly sailed.

For many a long year I felt quite guilty and sad at being unable to return his little blue torch and knew he would have been very disappointed, and would dismiss me as being untrustworthy, not knowing of the difficulties involved in attempting to carry out his request.

Four years later and now a seafarer myself, I served aboard a vessel discharging in Bombay, and ashore one evening I happened upon a small roadside bazaar displaying odds and ends, including a number of small torches exactly like the one in my City boat memories. I bought a blue one which, I noted included a new battery. Probably with the original in mind, but also for reading the log at night time en route to the wheel house, and with it being so useful, I left it lying on the table in our tiny seaman's cabin.

Next day on deck, hearing a hullabaloo I made my way to the cabin where an Indian bum boatman had been caught with a long, stout hooked wire stealing clothes, cigarettes, etc. through the open porthole in our cabin. The few things he had taken were quickly returned, however, I discovered my little blue torch had disappeared. Though the dockside policeman questioned and searched him time and time again at my insistence, the robber denied any knowledge of the torch. Even after a thorough cabin inspection by me and mates it was never seen again.

Yes, II know what you're cynically thinking, and I've dismissed the same silly conclusion myself. But even so, I wonder if it was possible that, no it couldn't be, for I don't believe in coincidences nor ghosts.

**A Spit in the Ocean**

Bored with painting the boat deck rails I spat in the Pacific Ocean, not a great deal, but never-the-less it all helps. Then I marshalled all the majestic powers of my elementary school education to try answering some puzzling questions. There's an awful lot of that water stuff sloshing around, where did it all come from in the first place? Well, I thought, maybe there wasn't such a lot; maybe it was my brain that was so small it just couldn't grasp large amounts of anything, such as the galaxies.

Then I got very profound. If I had no mind nor had anybody else, not even creatures or whatever, to analyse and interpret information, could the stuff be there if it wasn't appreciated? You would think yes, but I dunno, cos' I'm using consciousness to approach that question and that's cheating. In various focsuls I can't recall any discussion along those lines <u>at any time</u>. No, even that's wrong. Surely there's not 'any other time', there's only 'now', it always has been and always will be now, there never was a past nor a future. Only this instant. Time's just an invented measure to satisfy our tiny earth bound inadequate minds. Surely there's only change, with things constantly rearranging themselves neither backwards nor forwards. Just changing continually. No beginning, no end.

I started to get a headache, with this unusual thinking business... then I was rudely interrupted. "Come on son. Get on with paintin' the bloody rails," growled the passing Bosun, not realising the serious earth shaking complexities I was grappling with. I then remembered as a youth being very impressed by an illustrated book called the "Rubiyat of Omar Khayam" which, for the first time made my cob-webbed brain start to function. Adding a little more spit into the Pacific I remembered an Omar verse,

Myself when young did eagerly frequent

Doctor and Saint and heard great argument,

*Bill Backshall*

About it and about, but evermore

Came out the by the same door as in I went.

I realised like him, clever arse, profound thoughts change nuthin'. So I dipped heavily into the red lead whilst continuing my painting and theorising. Omar wasn't led down the false trails of yesterday and tomorrow. He was concerned with the present moment before things change. No illusions for him, and now I recalled another verse.

How sweet is mortal sovereignty think some

Others, How blessed the Paradise to come

Ah! Take the cash in hand and waive the rest

Oh the brave music of a distant drum

Seize the moment

Anyway, I've always thought his mastery of lovely words an inspiration and are unsurpassed. I turned over a line or two in my mind before the Bosun returned. What could better these random lines?

Alas that Spring should vanish like the rose

That Youths sweet scented Manuscript should Close,

and

Come, fill the Cup, and in the Fire of Spring

## Around the Buoys

The Winter Garment of Repentance Fling...

**"I've finished red leading the rails Bose. Think the Second Mates got any headache aspirins?"**

**"LAY AFT"**

Different ships different long splices so they say and in a way it was confirmed by our most unusual Bosun'. Well groomed, well spoken, well-educated with a well cultivated moustache, he was given at times to issuing words and phrases that startled the simple deck gang. Phrases such as, "We will rendezvous on the boat deck at 1300 hours" and, "Are you desirous of retaining or alternating watches at each passage completion"?

Definitely not the average Bosun's remarks you expect to hear aboard a rusty tramp steamer such as the "Fort Richelieu" sailing out of Liverpool. Then again, as if to underline his individuality, after his day's work he would retire to his cabin amidships and spend the rest of the evening tapping away at what we later discovered was a typewriter. For we learnt through the catering grapevine he was a published author using his experiences at sea as a peg to base his novels on.

He viewed and treated the admittedly rough Liverpool deck hands with poorly disguised disdain and reserve, that generally we only cheerfully accepted from the Officers. He sniffed and wiggled his well cultivated moustache to indicate his suspicion that we were probably Neanderthal descendants, resulting in him keeping us at the proverbial boat hooks length away. The old 'Non-Frat' class barrier was in no danger of being dismantled from the man in question.

Being one of the deck hands concerned, and trying to be

open minded, I could to a degree understand his superior attitude, for we really were a motley bunch of poorly educated souls, destined by the structure of our society to be simple labourers with, in the main, drink being our only solace. A little self-examination confirmed we weren't candidates to become future knights of the realm, but be that as it may, like most human beings we still had basic good points if you cared to take soundings The Bosun obviously had no understanding of our social background history, nor did he wish to know, and by the same token, nor was there any admiring desire by ourselves to take an interest in his social standing and resulting viewpoint.

And so the trip progressed with the Bosun supervising, but with just as little social contact required with the deck crowd, just passing the necessary orders and instructions. The States, the Medie, East Africa, New Zealand, God knows where next, a typical London Greek tramping voyage relieved by the occasional port of call drink problems from the crew. Nothing serious, just simple drunken tomfoolery till we fetched up at Newcastle, N.S. Wales. Having completed discharging our part cargo we prepared for departure and 'turning to' we started to drop derricks, cover hatches etc.,

*Around the Buoys*

the usual rigmarole with the Bosun directing operations in his imperious manner.

An A.B. casually interrupted his concentration and addressed him with a query about an entirely irrelevant matter. For some unknown reason, the Bosun annoyed, struck him with his fist full force, knocking him down to the deck. People nearby, crew, dockers, repair men, etc, stopped their actions and looked on with incredulity, absolutely dumbstruck, hardly believing what they had just witnessed.

So unexpected, so unnecessary, so unreasonable. The Bosun, still obviously carried away with his red mist, now shouted" Does anyone else want some?" at the same time waving his fist in the air. Before anyone could respond to his sudden absurd invitation, and to the everlasting amusement of the crew, he dismissed them by roaring dramatically, "Lay Aft!!" Meaning we believed, for we men to finish work and retire to our stern end quarters.

This "Lay Aft", command was received with howls of laughter, disbelief and derision by the deck gang, for the order sounded like something from the dialogue of a colourful Hollywood blood and thunder epic, with Jolly Roger flags, striped jerseys, eye patches, parrots, and walking the plank stuff. It sounded so incongruous to be heard aboard an ordinary everyday freighter it could only be assumed his mind was possessed with some Treasure Island sea story of yore he was currently engaged in writing.

But those two words acted like a catalyst, they immediately

deflated the Bosun's previous superior authority and reduced him to a figure of ridicule. With it being lunch hour the Bosun retired to his cabin obviously to consider his next move. The deck gang in protest, decided to descend the accommodation ladder and to visit the nearby tavern along the quay continually chanting cheerfully in unison as they went, "Lay Aft!, Lay Aft!, Lay Aft!"

Normally this pub visit would have ended in a drunken orgy with the ship's Officers eventually persuading the crew to get back aboard, with some of the trouble makers being logged. But this time a deep psychological pendulum had swung dramatically for in the pub the deck hands were now seriously discussing the matter, the outcome being. "He'll be hoping we get drunk now, go adrift and cause trouble, which would overshadow his own stupid behaviour. Let's carry out the opposite and give him something to write a true seafaring story about". This met with general agreement with all hands walking back aboard at exactly 1pm, and immediately voluntarily starting once again to drop derricks, batten hatches down etc. without the Bosun being in attendance.

He eventually showed up, but was totally ignored whilst the men worked manfully completing the various tasks. In fact the crew worked harder, more soberly and in complete harmony for the Mate from that point on, quietly ignoring any authority from the now isolated man who, for the rest of the voyage carried out minor maintenance tasks alone. Eventually, completely deflated, he attempted to ingratiate

*Around the Buoys*

himself with members of the deck crew, by becoming very pleasant mannered but met only courteous responses.

During the remainder of the trip the men continued to work conscientiously whilst unsupervised, with the Chief Officer being quite happy and relieved to see things running along smoothly even without the Boson's direction. He knew had he insisted on the Bosun being reinstated the men would have insisted he be logged for assault, thus complicating things for the Master and himself.

The vessel eventually arrived quite peacefully in the river Clyde with a cargo of iron ore. The deck personal who had left Liverpool returned home with a reversal of roles. A troublesome, ill mannered, 'chip on the shoulder' bunch of rough seamen changed to a respectful, self-disciplined, hardworking crew. And an arrogant, condescending, superior Bosun returned a chastened, subdued, far more pleasant natured man. There is always basic goodwill latent in all parties, but it took those two small words, "Lay Aft!!" from windship days to overcome the prejudice.

**Telegraph Tension**

The bridge of the Ellerman's City boat was partially wrecked by a bomb that had struck the alongside warehouse and repairs were urgently underway for the vessel was due the join a convoy shortly and nothing must impede her voyage. Most repairs had gone satisfactorily, but sadly the telegraphs were ruined and replacements at such short notice were impossible to find. The only solution, the telegraph engineer suggested, was to fit available, but much smaller tug boat telegraphs.

Reluctantly the Master accepted them even with the knowledge they would require much more physical effort making them difficult to use. "Anyway, we can phone down for increased engine revs or whatever, if need be!" was his optimistic observation. Racing against time the telegraph engineers completed the fitting just as the vessel entered the locks outward bound.

Despite repeated insistent appeals by the engineers the Captain told them there simply wasn't time to go through the rigmarole of testing them thoroughly for tension etc, and to get their gear ashore quickly before they too joined the voyage. The two men reluctantly threw their tool bags onto the lock quay and hastily climbed down a rope ladder just as the ship got under way.

Later in the voyage and in the 'Meddie', a U-boat Commander was determined to find a juicy target for his last two tin fish and his prayers were answered as he lined up the City boat. However, the clear, calm blue waters soon disclosed the wake of his periscope alerting the ship's lookout. The Master immediately ordered "Full Ahead!" to the Third Mate at the telegraph, whilst bawling to the helmsman "Hard a Port!!" in no uncertain terms.

*Around the Buoys*

The Third Mate, very concerned about getting his feet wet, grabbed the telegraph handles and knowing of its deficiency put everything he had into ringing the stiff machine. The submarine Kapitan smiled knowingly as he spotted the sudden tell-tale billowing of smoke from the vessels stack disclosing engine movements, and he adjusted his sights to where the torpedo would hit ahead of the present position.

"You're too late now for speeding away Tommy!" he said, loosing off one of his precious deadly charge. Aboard the vessel the Master was concerned for his ship wasn't answering very quickly to his request for an increase in speed. In fact, she seemed to be stopping and to his further disbelief, she started trembling as the engines pounded pulling her astern.

"What the hell have you rung down Third?" he barked. "Full Ahead Sir! Definitely Full Ahead! But the repeaters answered wrongly!"

"Well something's come unstuck, we're a sitting duck now, she's going astern," replied a now resigned Master, awaiting disaster at any moment.

"Get the men up from down below," he ordered. After frantic seconds passed, an urgent cry came from the forecastle lookout, "Torpedo passing well ahead Sir!"

"What a lucky escape!" shouted the 'Old Man', "The bloody telegraphs are unreliable, so in future Third, use the telephone. Never mind those bloody tug things."

The German submariner disappointed, repositioned later and breathed "You won't fool me this time Tommy with you clever going astern tactic!" He aimed for where his quarry would be after going astern as before. The ships funnel belched smoke again indicating engine movements as he loosed off his last torpedo. Aboard the City boat the Third Mate shouted down the phone "Full Ahead!" and shortly after the lookout reported, "A torpedo passing well astern, Sir."

The German submariner turned for his home base a bewildered and disappointed man! The City boat Mater wasn't sure whether to curse or praise the tug boat telegraphs.

**Landfall**

Like most seafarers I've experienced nasty storms and also some time ago I had a few horrible missiles fired and dropped in my direction, with a few near misses that thankfully let me carry on breathing. But to be honest, I've only been desperately worried on a few occasions. Not that I'm brave, far from it, it's just that I think we're armour plated with a brash, youthful confidence at an early stage of our lives, 'It's always the other guy who's going to get it', or 'I'm alright Jack I'm inboard', and all that stuff, until later as we become a little older divorced from youthful confidence, things can change into something really worrisome.

## Around the Buoys

For you see I've never faced my present situation before, and now in the cold stark reality of it all, my mind seems reluctant to accept it is actually happening. What's that old saying about being stuck between the devil and the deep blue sea? Well, that was the thought that burns bitterly in my brain, and to be honest, it wasn't really deep blue, but nasty grey-brown stuff that sloshed around out there.

The flapping wet canvas slapped across my face stinging my eyes and fouling my mouth with its nasty taste as I poked my head through the "Marlin's" port wheelhouse opening. The canvas had long since been torn to shreds by the fierce south- westerly that howled through the remnants; still it would have to do what it had to do, for I'd be a fool to venture out onto the side deck even with a life line. Once over the side in this weather and that would be 'curtains'. Far better to stay inboard where I was safe and dry for just a little longer and where I could close my eyes to what would be inevitable shortly. Staring blindly through the driving rain, I knew roughly where the welcoming lights of my safe haven lay, but it was plain silly to expect a visual which would give me false encouragement and bolster my hopes.

Despondent, I accepted the fact there was little possibility of succour in that quarter, even the little diesel fishing boat "Thumper" which had rolled and bobbed ahead of me had long since disappeared from view and with it all contact with life on this planet. I questioned myself being so bloody dramatic, but that's how isolated I felt. In the first place I'd been a damn fool venturing out, with the forecast threatening gales with heavy rain. More so with being so ill-prepared, and I could now understand why seafarers called week-end small boat men 'Suicide sailors'.

Another disgusted glance at the lifeless engine reminded me that the only light left was the small torch I held, and I gripped it tighter as though it was the only friend I had left in the world. I kept trying to think of something positive, but annoyingly all that came to mind was the silly fact I'd finished off the hot coffee in the afternoon, for at that time all seemed calm and serene. Yes, come to think of it, that's exactly how I'd been misled to disregard the forecast, little realising just how quickly the weather can change around our coast.

I was now forced into accepting the fact that I'd be a lucky man to escape this tight spot without paying a heavy price, for the elements exact a tidy charge when treated with indifference and incompetence. She gave a nasty roll and I staggered across to the starboard side where I was lucky enough to finish up grabbing a stay, my heart was in my mouth for I knew I could easily have fallen over the gunwale. The thought of the icy waters covering me, made me break out into a sickly sweat, for I knew that particular fate was not too far away. However, I refused to think about that situation for a little longer.

My main worry was the frightening sound of water slopping around dangerously high in the bilges and I half-heartedly worked the semi-rotary, knowing I was fighting a losing battle. The stern tube was leaking worse than ever, and that

*Around the Buoys*

coupled with the torrential rain. And water she had already shipped was making the pumps efforts of little consequence. I began to acknowledge the fact it was getting too late to stay aboard.

My converted boat "Marlin", had originally been a lifeboat aboard my favourite vessel the "Hinakura", to be replaced by a low maintenance fibreglass version, and I always knew in the back of my mind that being of metal construction, she would go down quickly should she someday be overcome, unlike the older wooden craft which could probably stay afloat even after turning turtle, giving the occupants at least a chance of survival.

Another squall struck the "Marlin" and looking outboard I could sense the wind was veering putting her beam on, resulting in her starting to broach. Thoughts flooded through my mind. At times like this when faced with a dilemma, knowing I couldn't stay aboard much longer and also knowing that to jump over the side was to invite a certain drowning, it is natural to think of one's close loved family and friends, and regret the promises I'd made and forgotten. The visits I intended to make to sick and lonely folk, the love I meant to show and neglected to carry out. The extra care I could have taken, and even that animal charity I had sincerely promised to help, all those 'good intentions' I'd casually overlooked.

What is it they say? "The road to Hell is paved with them." Well, I've certainly laid a few flags along that particular highway in my time. Whatever, now I'd have to take my chances for there were no options left and with that final decision taken I tightened my oilskin, sou'wester, and sea-boot's Gathering every ounce of courage and knowing full well that within, a few minutes of plunging over the side, I'd almost certainly be drowned, or damn near drowned. But who would care? Apart from my wife that is, sadly not many people, and why should they? I hadn't shared their concerns as well as I could have in the journey through Life.

Anyway, it was too late for those sort of regrets. I realised I was only subconsciously attempting to find a way of putting off the moment of committal. Sliding the lee-side door open I stared out into the crazy night and the ferocity of the wind and driven rain took my breath away making my spirits hit absolute bottom. *'This is it,'* I thought and mumbling some half-forgotten prayer, I struggled onto the gunwale capping and steadying myself with the life-belt that lay on the wheelhouse top, I finally jumped committing myself into fates hands. I floundered and the water was unbelievably cold as it covered my face and hands and started to penetrate the openings of my clothes and rubber boots.

"God help me," I cried, I was damned near drowned already confusion reined in my brain as some outstanding parts of my life flashed before me in a jumbled procession. I felt near to tears, but determined to struggle on, self-preservation is a powerful instinct that won't be denied. I fought to control my panicking mind, attempting to censor out the terrible fear I felt as I concentrated upon Reggie's voice shouting to me from his fishing boat "Thumper", moored thirty yards along the canal bank.

"Nasty night Bill! We'll get drowned before we get anywhere near the pub for that late pint, and for Chrise sake, you've made a good start jumping right into that bloody great puddle!"

**Carpet Magic**

With great curiosity, he'd watched his Mother carefully cutting up discarded, but well washed garments into strips about an inch wide and two or three inches long, and this had carried on now for a couple of weeks. At times he would ask her what she was doing, but all he got in return was a smile and "Just you wait and see Bobby!"

Then things became a lot more interesting when, one evening, she brought home a length of burlap and a metal hooked needle of sorts, with which she started to tuck the strips half way through it leaving the two ends protruding. Intrigued, he watched her select various coloured strips one after the other and to his delight, slowly a pleasant pattern of circled flowers developed as she worked away tucking each piece into place.

Patiently, night after night his Mother never tired, even after completing her hard days cleaning work and then her own household chores and his admiration grew as the sacking was covered piece by piece until one triumphant evening the work of art was finished.

"Well, what do you think of your magic carpet Son?" his Mother asked cheerfully as she swept the bare floor by the side of his small bed and laid down the new colourful rug with some degree of pride. "It's marvelous Mam," he chirped. "It's the best carpet in all the world," throwing his arms into the air to endorse his admiration. Actually, it wasn't the best carpet in the world, but it certainly was the best carpet in the tiny terrace house in dockside Bootle where they lived, for it was the first and only one, most floors being covered with odd squares of lino upstairs, and simply left as scrubbed stone tiles downstairs, bare and cold.

"Good lad," smiled his Ma, pleased to see that her son appreciated her efforts, "But it's not a carpet really Bob, it's what folk call a rug."

"No Mam!! It's not a rug; I think it's the best carpet in all the world!" Fiercely defending his Mothers work piece, for the word 'Carpet' seemed more important than the horrible word 'Rug'.

Later, he realised his Ma was right, for his carpet really was a Magic one, and he could pretend he was in a plane or a train, even aboard his Dad's ship, anything was possible sitting inside the circle of flowers on his Ma's carpet. He could slide on it to the window where he could see a battery of cranes and sheds that was the Gladstone dock, and he would then

*Around the Buoys*

in his imagination visit those faraway places his Dad had told him about.

That was the dock where he had sailed from long ago, but his Ma had told him his Father had now docked safely in Heaven aboard his ship. Other isolated cameos from his boyhood, remained crystal clear in his mind, but that was the most vivid of the all, the fond memory of his loving Mother and her magical colourful carpet.

A squawk of seagulls brought him back to reality, and made him focus again on the view of the river from his favourite spot. *'Cripes! Daydreaming again about carefree boyhood days,'* thought Bob Medway, and coming down to earth he dragged himself into the present day, and it was, 'Just perfect, just a perfect day, absolutely brilliant' he appreciated, letting the sun warm his weathered face for he knew this was one of those special moments in a lifetime that register indelibly and make you wish those precious moments could be frozen in time and last forever, *'especially for us older ones,'* he added to himself with an ironic grin.

The lovely long day had been another of summers golden gifts and as it lengthened towards late afternoon, it was apparent that the flaming sunset with a couple of high posted white clouds would be a treasure he couldn't possibly miss. So, after his meal in his sheltered accommodation flat, he swung his binoculars over his shoulder, checked his pipe was well primed and grabbing his trusty walking stick, began a measured but determined saunter back to his favourite "Sunset Strip", a stretch of beach that gave panoramic views of the River Mersey and vague misty N Wales.

On the way mixed feelings crowded his mind, but he made no effort to direct his thoughts, letting them wander randomly, but the same time with a small part of his brain standing aloof and detached in a supervising manner, checking upon which direction they would take.

Generally, he found they were, they inclined mostly towards the melancholy side of things, but occasionally swinging to the cheerful and appreciative emotions. This time he found they picked up the threads of his earlier daydream of his Mothers flowery magic carpet and he already found that by some coincidence when he gambled on a horse with, or something associated with the name, Carpet, he quite often won a tidy sum of money, especially when needed.

A little rest now, for he had reached the fancy flower bed at the edge of the shore-side green he called 'Plymouth Hoe' and here he could take his first view of the Mersey river eager to see if there were any vessels of interest in sight. But sadly as usual these days all he could see were a couple of small craft and a solitary container type vessel outward bound abreast the Gladstone Wall…

Not like in his day when, at the flood the channel would be full of various types of shipping, magnificent liners, cargo ships, tankers, dredgers, tugboats, coasters etc., but he pulled himself up short, "Come on Bob, that's all gone, and we know it, let's get back to present day life."

*Around the Buoys*

Soon he anchored at his favourite spot, and by perching his bottom on the low concrete wall, the next thing was to light his pipe and then he could settle himself and enjoy the wonderful sunset that was being presented to him and the other appreciative on-lookers peppered around him. Again as he drank in the serenity, the beauty and colours, his mind got itself out of gear again and he let it wander off on its own, letting it have its own head, as it were, like a horse grazing, wandering around as fancy took it.

Here I am just sitting here watching the sun set, as its probably setting on me, and I'm wondering what it's all about? Why does life play these tricks on us? They tell me I'm now 78, but it was only yesterday I was 8 or 18 or 38 and Oh yes!, at 38 I realised I knew everything, had been everywhere, and still had all the time in the world spread out before me, and now a day later they've got the cheek to tell me it was all in vain for it was only a bloody dream!

What a load of old rope! Bob, detached, smiled at the course his mind was taking, but he let it carry on unchecked. Funny things dreams aren't they? Occasionally you get a vague, fleeting feeling you partly remember one and the situation it created, but it remains just out of complete recall. And the more you try to recapture it the more it slips beyond reach like a bar of slippery soap in the bath.

I suppose that with every second that passes everything becomes a future dream… but here Bob broke off his reverie for the container ship was almost abreast of him now, and he wanted to make a more determined effort to read its name.

Steadying the binoculars on the low wall, he began to make out the letters on the bows,

"Car, Carp, Carpetial!" and then he quickly identified the Italian ensign flying at the stern. "Carpetial! Jeez, what a coincidence." He seemed to be haunted by that sort of name all through his life.

"Well, Well, Well! What a laugh. Still coincidence or not, it landed me on easy street quite a few times through my life. I wonder, could this be another good omen?" The name again made his memory flash back to his earlier dream about the carpet down Marsh Lane, his Ma's home made one with its ring of flowers that took him anywhere in the world just like his Dad's ship.

Following the line of his thoughts, Bob turned towards the line of North Liverpool docks trying to locate the Brocklebank Dock, where he'd joined an old tramp steamer called the "Fort Richelieu" with a bunch of cheerful but unruly local seaman which again had enmeshed him in another Carpet incident.

With the setting sun now burning strongly on his face, he closed his eyes and simply let the memories flood back into his mind, like a spring flood tide swamping everything else. With WW2 not long over, shipboard discipline had relaxed somewhat resulting in the ships departure being delayed somewhat though drunken dock road behaviour leaving home. The vessels first port of call was Bombay, where the crew had again caused a few problems by getting out of hand through drink. Nothing serious, just drunken tomfoolery, but still it didn't make a good impression on the Bridge Staff.

Whilst the ship was working her cargo, the Master and a few of the Officers, through the agent, had purchased a number of large, heavy patterned carpets, knowing that full well on their return to the UK, they would sell at a tidy profit, considering the shortage of such luxuries caused through the war years. Unfortunately, before returning straight home as was expected, the ship had been ordered to Auckland, N. Zealand, so the carpets were stored for safety in a forward mast house.

On the passage, bad weather was encountered crossing the Indian Ocean, with a few heavy seas being shipped through the mast house vents soaking the carpets. As soon as the fine weather returned, the deck hands were busily employed draping the large carpets over the dropped derricks where they soon dried out and with a stiff brushing to remove any salt they were found to be as good as new again.

During this process the foredeck resembled an Indian carpet bazaar, and in better spirits now, the Officers decided to store them out of the weathers way, in a small locker on the poop deck. The carpets were now out of danger weather-wise, but they were now exposed to other dangers, for the locker wasn't quite as secure as the mast house, a feature noted by the sticky fingered deck and black gang.

Bob broke off from his memories, opened his eyes to check on the container ships progress, and satisfied with its position carried on with his daydream. The tramp steamer finally reached its destination, Auckland, but without much joy for the crew, the Captain having refused any form of money to give them a run ashore, this being a form of punishment for their earlier unruly behaviour.

This was especially trying for Bob, whose 21$^{st}$ birthday fell on the next day and to add insult to injury, he found he'd been made night watchman whilst in harbour. He was now more or less out of touch with things, being asleep most of the day and on duty mainly alone through the night.

The vessel lay uneasily at her moorings during the first day in harbour. The crew obviously sullen with no funds to slake their thirst after a lengthy period at sea, but late afternoon the following day something happened that had the ships complement agog with curiosity and excitement, none more so than 'Birthday Bob.' A brewers dray drew up at the ships side and parked there laden with crates of ale, casks of beer, and a couple of boxes of spirits. Soon the deck hands swung a derrick outboard and then landed the surprise cargo on No Four hatch. Much to the delight of the crew, and the amazement and puzzlement of the Officers. No questions were asked as all hands helped themselves, through the day and night the liquor was consumed in large quantities with plenty remaining for the next day's entertainment. The only unhappy people aboard being the Officers, who wondered how the hell the enterprise was funded.

The next morning they were to find the answer, the Chief Officer discovered the locker on the poop deck had been

*Around the Buoys*

forced open and the carpets no longer in evidence. The local police were soon on the scene, and Bob recalled how his shipmates were questioned at length, with some of them still being half drunk and unable to answer properly. However, a fireman, two deckhands and two stevedores were arrested and taken away. Later the police returned with the stolen carpets, and the sailors, but minus the stevedores.

As the Master joked later in private, he had the three men responsible "On the carpet!" logging them heavily and had their discharge books endorsed with a D.R. They were not imprisoned, for the Master didn't want to lose members of his crew, but he logged all the others for joining in the business.

Altogether, not a bad outcome really. The Officers had their carpets, the police had their men, and the crew still had a few drinks left over. Nobody was more pleased though than Bob, because the Captain decided not to charge him, for with being on night watchman duty he couldn't possibly have had anything to do with the offence. Still, he had the best 21$^{st}$ Birthday celebrations anybody could possibly have wished for at no expense. "Carpets to the rescue again," as Bob put it, realising once more that quite a few times they had mysteriously come to his aid. "Well, just a coincidence I suppose, though it seemed to be getting a regular carpet thing!" The container ship was now starting to swing to port off the Formby Point and Bob let his mind drift on, recalling some of those other carpet episodes in his life all of them with helpful endings he noted gratefully.

'Oh yes!" One in particular had been that coincidence bet on a horse called 'Carpet Bagger', which had netted him a very goodly sum at a most helpful time. He didn't even know what a 'carpet bagger' was. Something like an American salesman, well, something like that. But the most rewarding one had occurred after he'd been retired for a year and he'd begun to realise he wasn't as well placed as he thought he would be financially. Things were getting to be a little tight.

It was then he was delighted to receive an invitation to the retired ex-seaman's Christmas Dinner, which was to be held in the Atlantic Hotel downtown. Sadly though, before he'd even had a drink with his old shipmates, he'd tripped and fallen heavily down a couple of steps in the hotel Foyer. The cause of the accident was obvious to the staff and friends alike, for a metal strip that covered the edges of two lengths of carpet had become loose, allowing the material to pucker up and Bob was the first person to suffer from the result.

A badly fractured Femur had him laid up in hospital for weeks and though the ensuing court case against the insurance company was a long drawn out affair, it was a foregone conclusion that Bob would be awarded substantial damages. The amount he received settlement was generous to say the least, and he knew he was on Easy Street for the rest of his life. Of course he paid a price with a permanent limp, but that aside, somehow a carpet had again solved some worrying times.

The vessel 'Carpetial' was now a smudge on the horizon getting beyond the Queens Channel, and Bob, still letting his

*Around the Buoys*

thoughts drift on, grinned as he reminded himself of a silly ambition he'd long held to write a short story of how his Ma's magic flowered circle carpet had watched over him and seen to it he'd always been provided for with money and good luck. "Nonsense really," grinned Bob, "carpets can't help you really I suppose."

It's just that coincidence plays a part in all things in life and we are tempted to see more in them than is sensible. Still, it would make a good hook for a short story. Suddenly, he realised the last vestige of the sun had now declined beyond the Welsh coast and as he gathered himself together preparing for his slow walk home, he began to feel a chill creeping over him and it struck him as odd, for although he'd lost the direct sun's warmth, the evening shouldn't have cooled that quickly. However, he stood up and turned himself southbound on his new course.

"Blast! Will I ever forget those damned seafaring terms?" He mocked himself, "People will start to skit you if you persist with them, so give them a miss Medway! Anyway, I'll take it easy to the edge of the 'Ho' where the flower patterns are, for my first little rest."

The Crosby Herald was very sympathetic with its report in the weekend edition. The headlines of a small column reading Elderly Ex-Seaman's Death. It gave a caring description of how the body of Robert Medway (78) was found lying on a thick bed of carpeted flowers at 'Sunset Strip', just within sight of the river, where he liked to spent most of his spare time since retiring from seafaring.

He appeared to have fallen, but landed gently, for the thick carpet of flowers had cushioned his fall; sadly leaving him nestled in the circled pattern of the flower bed.

**Pier Headin' Lazy Days.**

Lazin' on this waterfront seat, knowin' that my life is near complete

Checkin' on the Liver clock and the tall ships in the Albert Dock.

Time keeps driftin' right on by, like clouds that billowed in my troubled sky

Figured it's a watch too late to pray, I'm just 'Pier Headin' lazy days away.

Sepia flash of times gone by, dockside streets with pavement flags bleached dry

No one said but life was pretty hard when Pa had worked the China and Cunard.

Cobbled roads and warehouse walled where the Yankee dollar seldom called

Cash was penny tight but what's to say, I'm just Pier Headin; lazy days away.

## Around the Buoys

Some Sunday rest for hard worked Mam, Pa took us on the 16 tram

Saw the liners grace the Landing stage, sailing that Blue Riband age.

Feet behind the brass line strip when the crowded ferry moored each trip.

Lately things have slipped astray, its best Pier Headin' troubled times away.

Muddy Mersey slipped astern, years of tramping oceans brings a yearn

Sweated in the tropic sun, shivered Winter North Atlantic run.

Stories of my Spring tide days, but who's to care what this old drifter say?

Let's hoist a wistful smile and "Hey, it's no sin just wastin' hours away".

Memory drunk and humming song, got it figured where it all went wrong

Youthful dreams have turned out duds, our placid river simply ebbs and floods.

Best take the sun and salt air breeze enjoy the past and live what's left at ease.

Past caring now my hairs turned gray, philosophising lazy days away.

Why don't you sign and watch your river flow? It'll pluck your tender heart strings so. Makes you dream of times apast, when your tide was truly flooding fast

With plans for love and life's desires that smouldered with your youthful fires.

Relive them once again OK, then get them right while musing hours away

Shoe swingin' on this waterfront seat, feel better now my preaching's near complete

I've watched the world go walking by, all with hidden worries in their *Sky*.

They should drop their hook and follow me m Pier Headin' lazy thoughtful days away.

**Watch Below**

I began telling Spike it reminded me about a similar case, but he immediately replied "Oh no! Here we go again 'Swingin' the Lamp.'"

"No!" I answered, a little miffed. "Every word of this tale is true, I swear, though I doubt you'll believe the end like a lot more folk." His valued wrist watch had snagged and dropped

*Around the Buoys*

off climbing over the gunwale capping. Luckily, with my small converted boat being shored up on the Gladstone quayside he soon retrieved it from the ground. I continued. We were about to enter Halifax on the "Cavina" when a dozen or more fishing smacks got in our way, some apparently with nets down making things difficult for the Captain to manoeuvre.

"Keep your eyes open over there Smith," he ordered my pal Johnny, who had been waiting in the wing of the bridge to relieve me at the wheel. Soon all was clear but as he withdrew his head from the cabin port window sadly his wristwatch strap caught on the window stay peg, stretched, and then broke. He desperately tried to grab it, but unfortunately he had to watch it fall 30/40 foot or so to the water, disappearing with a 'plop!' He was absolutely heartbroken. "Whatever will the wife say? She'll go bonkers having bought it especially for our Wedding anniversary!"

Saying this he looked hopefully at a trawler left wallowing in our wake, but having to face the truth that it was finito.

I continued with my story to Spike, despite his cynical expression. Next afternoon Johnny and myself took a walk ashore in the port, but the freezing weather soon had us heading back to the vessel. En route we were both surprised to see a high class chip shop/diner. "Didn't know they had chippy's over here!" we agreed, and of course the smell of the place immediately made us hungry. I wanted to wait to get aboard to eat, but Johnny decided to settle for a nice fresh cod and chips for an advert boasted "Fresh Fish Caught

Daily", and he soon came out with a fancy carrier like you get over there. He couldn't wait to get stuck in.

"Now listen Spike," I broke off to speak to him, "I know you won't believe this part of the story, like a lot more folk I've told it to, and you'll probably call me a right romancer and liar, but every word I'm about to tell you is true, so help me thingy."

"Anyway," I carried on, as Johnny took a ravenous bite and chewed happily, but on his second bite he stopped with a look of shock, put his hand to his mouth as I said, "I know you won't believe it, but guess what was in that mouthful?" I paused then continued,

"It was ----"

But here Spike interrupted me to explode incredulously,

**"Don't tell me!! I know!! His Bloody Wrist Watch!!"**

"No." I replied, "Nothing but a fish bone, you bloody fool!!"

## S.O.S

At the beginning of WW2, aged 14, I started serving my time as an apprentice Joiner, but being employed by a small family firm meant when required, I was occasionally sent to work with the bricklayers, jobbers and also to my dismay, an old painter. With the war creating a shortage of tradesmen he had come out of retirement and though 77 he was still a master craftsman.

Named William Michael Peers he was partially deaf, he was physically crouched over like a question mark, and smoked thick twist tobacco in a foul anti-social pipe. He often chewed the tobacco, which yellow - stained the edges of his already untidy moustache, but I feel a close description of that chewing habit is unfit to publish, even for hardened readers. Also, his steering gear was suspect for he repeatedly bumped into anybody who walked with him or neared his vicinity. A seafarer would have recommended he carry fenders either side. He was also the owner of a dry cackling laugh that he employed when he attempted one of his own unfathomable jokes.

When I was begrudgingly sent to work with him, being a fully paid up member of the "Smart arse, Know it all Youth Club", I dismissed him constantly as a "Soft Old Sausage", but he didn't let my arrogant sarcasm bother him. He just smiled and replied quietly, "Don't worry Bill, you'll find out."

At that stage I never understood nor found out what he meant, but again, I didn't give much thought to anything he said, 'cos if you think back carefully, the world is full of SOS's like him especially when you're sixteen.

He had a small paint shop in the corner of the work yard where he would mix his Venetian reds, Brunswick greens, Yellow ochre's or whatever, whilst smoking his horrible pipe and rubbing the excess paint off his brushes on the door prior to cleaning them. This rubbing resulted in large bulges inches thick forming when the passage of time turned into years, and he was always eager and proud to exhibit them to visitors. Slowly I began to appreciate how masterful he was at his trade and began subconsciously to accept his techniques which stood me in good stead in later years.

On reaching eighteen, I prepared to join the Merchant Navy establishment at Gravesend. Sea School, and as I packed my tools on my last Saturday morning before departing, Billy came across and after enveloping me in the usual cloud of foul pipe smoke, he shook my hand and wished me well. He was the only person who did.

"Soft Old Sausage", I thought, but not as dismissive nor as cynical as before, and we both knew that it would be the last time we would meet. "Don't worry Bill," he said with a twinkle in his eye and with his cackling laugh, he added for the last time, "You'll live to find out." Another one of his bloody obscure jokes, I thought.

Well the war ended, not that I frightened many Germans into surrendering. In fact quite a number of them frightened me, so enjoying the seafaring life, I carried on for quite some years and then took marine employment along the line of the Liverpool docks, until one morning I awoke to realise somebody or thing, had fiddled with the calendar and I was now aged seventy- seven and well retired.

Ironically, it struck me I'd reached the old painter's age. I was very annoyed but try as I may, I couldn't alter that fact, so I decided to enjoy my freedom from work by visiting some of the old places that had figured in my earlier life. Places such as the terrace street where I was born, the street corner where I stood with my mates, other houses my family had lived in, my old school, the railway bridge incline where my father walked we kids on Sunday morn' to view in the distance the Gladstone dock where he was employed. Sadly, quite a number of the places I visited had disappeared or been rearranged thanks to the Luftwaffe, but I still enjoyed the nostalgia of the areas.

Late one dark November dismal afternoon, my target was to view the old contractor's yard where I had served my time all those year ago. Though still a builders firm it was now rather neglected and deserted when I arrived. Through the gloom I could see the saw bench area, next to the joiners workshop, the glass cutting dept. the retail shop, and outside I took in the old painters shed with Billy's proud showpiece the paint bulged door.

After a quiet period of reflection, I said a mental nostalgic, *"Happy days, but Good-bye,"* and turned quickly about to head for home, unfortunately as I did, a youth riding a bicycle on the pavement ran into me, more or less knocking me to my knees. Before I had time to harangue him with a few well-chosen words he beat me to it, and riding off into the gloom, with the smartness and arrogance of youth, he shouted "Soft Old ****!!"

No, he didn't use my descriptive word of 'Sausage' that I employed when referring to Billy, the old painter, something rather more obscene but still applicable, I suppose. Confused by the swiftness of the accident, I gathered myself together, then struggling to my feet, I began to get amused by the significance of it all and instead of being upset as you would expect, I found myself smiling wryly at old Billy's enigmatic forecast that I now suddenly clocked onto, the penny dropped!

Well, I walked away some distance from the yard, only to get an irresistible urge to look back again at the painters shed. However, you're probably wrong in what you're thinking, for I failed to see a ghostly figure crouched at the paint shop door sniggering, "Don't worry Bill, you'll find out!!" Which, I agree, would have made a good ending to my story, though a little bit contrived. But, between you and me, I'm bloody sure I got a whiff of thick twist tobacco smoke, and I <u>definitely</u> heard a dry cackling laugh.

**Pot Black**

As an impressionable young man during that distant war, I was brainwashed into believing that all our enemies were crazy, uncaring, dangerous, thieving, etc., everything that's not nice and peaceful, as opposed to ourselves, we who were seemingly perfect.

Later on, I found that after hostilities ceased it didn't seem to matter to our leaders what we think about those self-same folk, even when we find our ex enemies really aren't a great

## Around the Buoys

deal different from ourselves. With this in mind it reminds me of a straw blown in this enlightening process.

O.K, so this happened a long time ago, but so too did your memories, that's how life is. Anyway, during a voyage we'd arrived at Genoa immediately after the end of that dreadful war and through an illegal transaction with some shore side Mafia gangsters, concerning a valuable ships mooring rope, we finished up having thousands of Lire to celebrate in the city centre, not that they amounted to a great deal.

As the evening wore on we ended up in the bar of a fine hotel that had been requisitioned by the Army. A drunken cheerful night drew to a close as we discussed 'Blighty' to war weary hometown soldiers, eagerly awaiting de-mob after serving abroad for years. Finishing up outside on the pavement in the balmy night air, we continued to answer their eager questions about current life back home in the 'Pool. I soon realised that I had neglected to visit the toilet before leaving. Worried, I looked around and across the road and spotted a deserted unlit old cottage of sorts surrounded by shrubs and railings. It seemed out of keeping with the more modern buildings around the area, but with nature now demanding increasing attention, I decided to ease the pressure over there and excusing myself to the company nipped over the road to skulk in the dark shelter of the place.

Being in a recently enemy country, it didn't seem to matter too much about observing conventions. I prepared myself, but looking up I was surprised to espy a large notice attached to the cottage wall which I managed to read as my eyes became accustomed to the darkness.

**"In this cottage in the year of our Lord 1451, Christopher Columbus, the great seafarer was born."** Embarrassed and ashamed at approaching the great man's birthplace with impure intentions and apologising to him mentally, I hurriedly excused myself and searched for another berth further down the road.

The side door of a small building opened and an elderly gentleman beckoned me with a few words of Italian, "Il cabinetto?" or something like that. Obviously he'd watched me and realising my embarrassment, invited me in and indicated the toilet door. Thanking him gratefully, I returned to my shipmates, but en route, I began to evaluate our own robbery, drunkenness, uncaring and greedy behaviour as opposed to our enemies, and it gave me a more balanced appreciation of the first paragraph of this story. An understanding that life certainly isn't all as one sided as we are sometimes led to believe. In fact, the kettle and the pot are often both black and often both white.

**Sling Your Hook**

The M.V. "Hinakura" lay light ship at the South Canada dock and I sat on the bitts enjoying my lunch hour admiring my vessel which, whilst awaiting a loading berth, had various repairs and alterations taking place aboard. My interest was taken by a small lorry arriving laden with a sling of T&G planed boards. It stopped under a yard arm derrick positioning itself ready for the timber to be winched aboard.

There seemed to be a lengthy pause and discussion on deck about who would go ashore to sling it, but eventually an elderly, portly workman appeared to have been selected and awkwardly descending the steep gangway approached the vehicle. Being a ship repair worker, he didn't look very confident as he boarded the lorry and prepared to sling the timber.

Having had personal worrisome experience of slinging dangerous slippery planed boards such as those, I was concerned when he simply wrapped a rope sling around the cargo, timber hitch style, and hooked it onto the derricks lowered runner. A cargo net would offer a safer lift and I considered suggesting one to the man. However, the winch quickly took the slack, then began to heave away.

Being a light ship there was quite a distance for the sling to reach deck level but it only managed six or seven feet before the perpendicular boards, as I feared, slipped and carried away plunging into the dock between the quay and the ships side. Ironic cheers, hurtful comments, and smart alec advice from the deck didn't seem to help matters, for the elderly man called Bob, who now embarrassed, surveyed the lovely new timber boards floating in the water.

Luckily, there was a steel ladder built into the quay side wall near the floating cargo and he slowly climbed down and started to fish out the reachable pieces. I decided to help the man by taking the pieces as he passed them up from the water level and we successfully rescued the majority.

The remainder were out of reach, so Bob now returned to the quay and taking off his shoes and socks, rolled up his trouser legs as high as possible. He then descended the ladder again, this time with his bandy white legs well into the murky dock water, and this enabled him; with the aid of a short piece to reach the remaining boards. To assist him, I climbed down the ladder a few rungs to better take the pieces from him. Just on completing the task he suddenly gave a loud squeal and began shouting and cursing incoherently.

Thinking I had inadvertently stood on his fingers as they clutched the rungs, I hurriedly climbed the few steps back up to the quay followed by the cursing gentleman. About to apologise, I was cut short as he immediately as he started performing some sort of one footed dance around the quay hopping here, there and everywhere, at the same time hollering, "Gerrimoff!!"

I was perplexed until I suddenly spotted what was causing his startling performance. A really large crab was firmly attached to the big toe of his right foot and was obviously nipping him painfully. Around he danced trying to get the damned thing off, but being rather portly, he found it wasn't that easy. The more he cavorted the more gales of laughter ran down from his mates on deck who were in stitches at his discomfiture.

*Around the Buoys*

The scene was reminiscent of seaside picture postcards with fat ladies and red nosed gentlemen.

The crab seemed determined to hang on to what it obviously thought was a tasty dinner, but finally an exhausted Bob managed to release it and throw it back into the Canada Dock. After drying himself and refitting socks and shoes, we commenced loading the T & G timber into a cargo net sling hoping this time for better luck.

Bob had now settled down, and seeing the funny side of things slyly winked at me and remarked, "We'll never get 'board' on this job!!"

**Piped Aboard**

Sunday morning saw me aboard a Mersey ferry boat discovering a grating that gushed hot oil smelling air. "That's the engine room," explained Father. Peering down I could only see a surprising abundance of pipes stuck everywhere, and being a clever child, the suspicion rooted that engine rooms appeared to be overpopulated with the enigmatic things.

Leaving school I gained ship repair employment assisting a telegraph fitter, and to complete the maintenance programme I would attend the engine room repeater answering his bridge commands for efficiency. Down amongst all manner of frightening wheels, cogs, and nasty machinery gubbins.

I once again cynically eyed the pipe phenomena, fathoms of the stuff en route from somewhere and disappearing to elsewhere. Common sense convinced me there was no need for so much pipery, small, big, going up, coming down, hot and cold, you name it and it would be busy piping itself around a corner, passing overhead or disappearing mysteriously through a bulkhead. Dormant childhood ferry suspicions were reawakened and confirmed and questioning whether all vessels suffered from this inexplicable complaint I determined to search for the truth.

Trained at Gravesend Sea School, I commenced seafaring and

later departing Lourenco Marques on a vessel covered with coal dust, the Bosun, preparing for a good deck wash down, said to me, "Nip down below and ask the Gingerbeer for water on deck!"

Bravely descending into the noisy alien world I successfully hand signalled the request.

Though it was an American built ship it was the same old story as I glanced cynically at those absurd pipes, nodding knowingly as I confirmed the engine/ boiler rooms of the world were indeed seriously overpiped. Questioned about the pipe plethora, the Engineer sheepishly signalled deafness and embarrassed, hastily retired to camouflage himself amongst his mechanical scenery. Ashore nowadays, and uninfluenced by conspiracy theories, I can report exclusively to the "Masthead" that an old fitter once employed by Camel

Lairds ship building yard, recently confessed the truth to me on his death bed.

Answering my investigative pipe saturation questions he broke down, then secretly and curiously winking and smiling at his wife, whispered, "Bill you must agree ships do need a lot of pipes, but in the builders yard fitters installing the new complex systems regularly get confused and lose track of which pipes are which and where the dickens their bound for. Fearing dismissal, they abandon unidentified pipes around some dark corner and begin anew.

"Pipes multiply when other tradesmen fitting more, also lose track of things and covertly weld the abandoned ends behind any old tank or boiler and start again. Many pipes you see are of this virgin variety, never used, but be warned!! This is a closely guarded trade secret. Keep it quiet or the pipe fitters may finish you off around some dark corner too." Saying this, he drew his finger dramatically across his throat. Then, stifling a gurgle, he choked fitfully and I feared he was about to drag his anchor. Luckily he recovered, but I again caught him winking and smiling slyly to his wife, which puzzled me, until I cleverly realised it signalled his relief at sharing his terrible burden with me.

Mindful of that murderous threat I vowed to keep his dark secret, confidential, but now, realising I'll be visiting no more nasty engine rooms and also not many fitters are piping on ships nowadays, I've bravely decided to pipe up and expose this shameful trade practice exclusively in this book.

*Bill Backshall*

**Looking Astern**

Have you fired an old coal burner till your back bone starts to creak,

Have you scaled the never ending rust on a tramping London Greek?

Have you snatched your dinner piecemeal waiting on the main saloon

Then pearl dived all those dishes, polished every knife, fork, spoon?

Have you stood a frozen lookout 'cross the Winter North Atlantic

Till your eyes grow sore and reddened, did the weather drive you frantic?

Did you slave the Galley every day preparing every course

Whilst the vessel rolls and pitches like a fairground hobby horse?

Have you lay awake with heavy eyes as your bunk rolls side to side

And fore and aft and up and down like a seaside dipper ride?

You lost all hope of getting sleep before your 12 to 4

## Around the Buoys

Did you curse and swear you'd take a job on a farm X miles inshore?

Did you learn what worry's all about on some black and stormy night

When you'd closed the land and failed to fix that bloody costal light?

Did you call the 'Old Man' which he'd hate, or trust yourself to fate?

At times you wished you were somewhere else and not a Second Mate.

In the boiler room and sweating with the temp on 'one-one-oh'

Have you tried in vain to trim the vents to catch the slightest blow?

Did your prickly heat kick off again once you reached the coast of Spain?

Have you cursed the 'Jaspers' in the mess, cleaned bilges after grain?

Maybe your Wife or Mother would figure in your thoughts

As you lay discharging oil drums in some God forsaken ports?

Were you just a wishful dreamer and did you gullibly believe

Those rumours that the vessel would be home for Christmas leave?

But when you've stowed your discharge book, both anchors down ashore

It's then you get to thinkin' about the great things not the poor.

True shipmates that you've sailed with their humour and their tales.

The Indian Ocean smooth as glass and those dhows with lateen sails.

The flying fish, the runs ashore, all bubble back to mind.

The Southern Cross and phosphorus, the green luminescent kind.

The 'Channels' at the voyage end and the 'Welcome home' were bliss.

Such thoughts will leave you bittersweet and nostalgically you'll miss.

The "Hardship" even with its faults and agree in light of this

We're still the proudest men its true, for it bestows a certain poise.

To have served the Merchant Service it sorts the men out from the boys.

*Around the Buoys*

**Lucky Star Boat**

Maybe it was because he was from Toxteth and I was from Bootle, or maybe not. More than likely it was because I was the man who relieved him on the next watch. Whatever the reason, Bob Medway certainly singled me out to make my life a drag, to say the least.

We were only a few days into the voyage aboard the 'Tacoma Star' when he began his stupid actions, unbeknownst to me at first. One of his earlier tricks was when I relieved him at the wheel; he would give it a few fast turns ether way immediately before I entered the wheel house. Then it would take me five minutes to get her back on course and settled down. The Mate after looking at the wake, would remark sarcastically "Are you signing your initials in the ocean for starters?" I tried to blame the last helmsman but it didn't seem to be accepted.

Then one day whilst painting the boat deck bulkheads my pot of paint got mysteriously knocked over causing the Bosun to give me a good old rollicking. I had an idea Bob did it purposely unseen, but he reported to the Bosun it was all my fault for leaving it where it was a hazard.

Again, as the voyage developed he would switch the rope yarns on the soogie bucket to the fresh water one causing me to get nowhere fast with the expected amount of paintwork cleaned, all sorts of little things that had the Mate and Bosun giving me the old fish eye.

And so things went on with me trying to fathom out why he was doing these annoying things to me, but reaching no explanation. Once when I'd been eye splicing some rope snotters he must have sneaked down the forepeak after me, unlaid some of the strands, then tucked them back wrongly so the Bosun would think I couldn't splice very well. But by this time the Bosun and Chief Officer knew somebody was playing spiteful tricks on me and it was obviously 'old Bob'. With a younger man I could have invited him out onto the hatch and sorted out our differences, whatever they were, but he was knocking on sixty odd and fisticuffs were out.

After discharging on the Aussie coast and loading at Wellington, we got ourselves homeward bound with him still mooring me up the creek at any given chance he got. However, I kept the locking bars on my temper until one night I really blew my top with his downright stupid lies. He told the Mate I refused to get out of my bunk after he'd called me for my watch, and he then accused me of being half an hour late with my look-out relief.

Why on earth he told such lies, nobody aboard could understand. Even the Mate knew he was a phoney by now and paid no attention to his accusations. But that last fib was 'it' with me. As soon as I was off watch I marched to the focsul and grabbing him around the neck, threw him back on his bunk, shouting "Leave me alone you stupid old man!! Or I'll wring your scrawny neck!" He just lay there sneering and said, "That's it Backy! Attack an old man like me, would you? Well, just you wait till my two hefty sons get a grip on you when we dock back in the 'Pool. Don't worry, I'll write and tell them you've duffed me up and for them to be ready and waiting to give you a good going over!"

So that was it then, he had craftily provoked me into giving him an excuse to alert his sons back home. When he pinned a photo of them up on the bulkhead to remind me what was coming, I could see they were like two walking warehouses, talk about hard case bouncers wasn't in it. For once I was in no hurry to reach the Mersey and get a glimpse of those Liver birds.

Though there was the usual nasty spitefulness, and more threats we managed to get home without major trouble, and late one afternoon we berthed at the West Gladstone Dock with me piping the quay apprehensively. Luckily, there was no sight of the two warehouses only dockers, shore gang men and tradesmen etc., so I breathed a sigh of relief and with the Bosun knocking us off after making fast the back spring I nipped smartly to the focsul and finished packing my gear ready to have it away home.

With handshakes to my other shipmates and the usual threats of meeting in the Caradoc next day after paying off, I grabbed my case and started to make my way to the accommodation ladder and hopefully safety. I was almost there when my heart started to beat ten to the dozen for striding along the deck were those two great warehouses, old Bob's sons, and one of them clocking me, growled like a ship's siren, "Hey lad! Are you Backy, who our old fellah told us about?" Trapped I reluctantly confessed "Yeh, That's me." I cursed my luck, if only I'd have been five minutes earlier I'd have missed them, but nevertheless I had to face things now.

"Right, we thought we'd recognise you," the foghorn sounded, "and we want a word or two with you to sort things out." They were that well-made I thought the ship would roll a bit as they made their way across the deck towards me.

Without boasting or blowing, but as a youth, I got bombed quite a lot, machine gunned once, fire bombed, and rocketed with V1's and V2's, and maybe with being so young I wasn't old enough to be really terrified and appreciate the danger I was in. But now I was well old enough to understand that real pain was fast approaching, for my knees were starting to give way beneath, and a visit to the toilet seemed a good idea.

Throwing my suitcase on the hatch, then peeling off my coat and chucking that down too, I thought, *'Well, I'll just try to defend myself as best I can, and hope an Officer or somebody comes along and stops the bloody mayhem before it gets too bad'*. As I struck up a pugilists pose balling my fists like those old fashioned boxers, I spoke up, "Now listen men, before you start, no matter what your old man said I've never laid a hand on him!" Famous last words came to my mind, *'would they be mine?'* The answer was the surprise of my life. The ships siren blared, "For Chrise sake, put your bleedin' hands down. You're posing there like Muhammad Ali in bad health.

*Around the Buoys*

And put your jacket back on before you get a bleedin' cold, you soft basket!"

I couldn't grasp what was going on but felt very relieved, and I did what he suggested. Then the other deep siren sounded off. "Now listen lad, our old fellah's a bloody nark, always has been and always will be, even the old lady's finally chucked him out. He regularly picks on some poor beetle early in a voyage then gets us to duff the poor sod up when they get back home, But lately we've clocked on to him and his little game realising he's the problem. So grab your gear and go and have a baby in the Caradoc, you deserve a pint or two after putting up with him all the trip. Don't worry we'll trim our old fellahs vents and sort him out!" Then they nodded, gave me a smile that would have frightened a grizzly bear, and indicated a kick up the stern end for their unloved father.

I shot down the gangway that quickly a smart arsed docker said, "Owe somebody aboard a few bob, whack?" and with a forced grin I bundled my gear into the taxi saying "Linacre Road pal!"

"Did ya have a good trip?" the driver enquired pleasantly. "Not really," I replied, but passing through the Gladstone gates and after a little thought, I added, "Still in the end she finished up being a Thank my Lucky Star Boat."

*Bill Backshall*

**Captain Crescent**

1930's. Carrying a precious newly home baked loaf and a few vegetables my Mother would send me to stay the weekend at my married sister's house in Waterloo a couple of miles walk away. With national mass unemployment those days, even the essentials of life were hard to attain, but Jimmy, my brother in law was a man determined to provide whatever he could. About 6am, we two would set off with a small hand cart soon to pass a row of lovely houses named 'Marine Crescent' facing the then busy River Mersey.

We would trek along the shore following the latest tide line. This was known locally as "Wreckin", or in other words beachcombing for anything of a value, new and old pieces of timber, coal lumps, paint pots, brushes, lengths of rope, even the odd sealed tins with various contents, in fact any items lost or thrown overboard. Good timber would be stored and hopefully sold, whilst the useless pieces would be sawn and burnt providing a glorious fire with the salt soaked content cleaning the soot from the flue. Trundling the loaded cart homewards over the soft golden sand was extremely tiring, but the reward was a cup of steaming tea and a piece of toast made at the cheering fire.

During the struggle homewards I would again admire the row of lovely houses with their long front gardens. Jimmy mentioned a certain famous ship's Captain lived in one, making me wish in my boy's mind, that I would try to grow up to be famous ship's Captain too and live in a splendid house like that. Many years later I discovered it was the tragic Captain Edward Smith of the doomed Titanic who had lived there and had of course died aboard his vessel.

Years later again, just a few houses away lived another famous ship's Captain, Johnny Walker, wartime hero of the H.M.S. Starling the 'Scourge of the U Boats', who died still a middle aged man, worn out through his victorious but exhausting Battle of the Atlantic efforts. This knowledge now brought bubbling to the surface of my mind conversations I'd heard from my elders of my Uncle, Walter Chapman, who, as a ship's baker, lost his life aboard the Liverpool passenger liner SS Vestris which foundered off the US coast in 1928 in heavy weather with a great loss of life both passengers and crew. Amongst those lost was Captain William Carey, who resided close by to the Crescent in Crosby.

I'm glad I only managed to get to be an A.B.

**Forward Motions**

Living right forward in an older type cargo vessel that is pitching in very heavy weather can create some interesting experiences, as I'm sure seafarers will appreciate. For instance, as the vessel's bows rise high to the lift of the seas, a person trying to descend a for'ad companionway ladder really needs to make an effort and literally force their way down. Normally of course, going down should be an effortless experience. Alternatively, a person normally requiring an amount of exertion to climb the ladder can be hurried up it without any effort, as if an unseen force is urging him upwards delivering him up top sometimes uncomfortably faster than he desired. These phenomena create a vague suggestion of gravity problems and weightlessness that are now common to modern day astronauts.

A similar interesting feature was suffered aboard an old coal burning freighter where we deck hands lived forward, focsul style, and where inconveniently the timeworn primitive plumbing was malfunctioning. This made visiting the for'ad toilets in the extremely heavy weather of the W.N.A. Another unusual experience. Visitors needing to occupy the faculties cubicles, would find that as the vessel's bows ascended to the lift of the mighty seas, the water in the toilet pan would disappear hurriedly, gurgling down to some deep dark unknown place, rather like an injured beast scuttling down to its bolt hole. Serenity would reign for a number of seconds, then, as the bows plunged to crash into the following trough, the water, as if hurriedly changing its mind, would make a hasty return storming maliciously back up into the pan, firstly filling it and then often flooding over the seat with its eager momentum.

Careful timing in every human action taken was vital for success in those circumstances. A second or two before the waters imminent return, an alert experienced occupant would cleverly dispatch himself from the seat with a mighty athletic spring whilst simultaneously attempting to secure his half-mast trousers and other 'at risk' features, shirt tail, belt

*Around the Buoys*

ends, personal appendages, to keep them clear of the nasty flooding waters. This action, given a little imagination, could remind one of a stricken jet pilot activating his ejector seat. It has been humorously suggested the inspiration for the said ejector seat may well have been conceived on just such an occasion, but we must underline that the suggestion is pure conjecture. Any unsuspecting tardy occupant caught unawares by such gravity dictates would rightly be refused entrance to the poorly ventilated main focsul quarters, being strongly directed to visit and make use of the nearby ablutions room.

**As a footnote, it was later found that in certain tropical zones flushing occasionally created interesting and pretty displays of sparkling phosphorescence in the receptacles especially at night time. However, hygienic consideration, sadly discouraged further scientific study in that direction.

**Compass Change**

Don't tell me that you've never let your mind ring slow astern.

Yes, right back to those voyages that held some sad concern.

I guess we've all siesta dreamed, deck chairing on the lawn,

'Bout could we cancel major faults, make a fresh start come the dawn.

Come on now let's be honest and I'm sure that you'll agree

Like me there were some stormy times when you ploughed an angry sea.

We'd truly like to track back in the roughest of those wakes

And try and slip the cable on our more miserable mistakes.

But I'm afraid they're done and dusted, with no chance for late aborts.

Say let's be more realistic, give a passage to wishful thoughts.

We're not the only ones regretful, who rue past bitter word?

So roll on our tomorrows, there untouched, (Well, so I've heard).

For memories are luxuries even the poorest can afford.

But the future gives us every chance to strike a sweeter chord.

Enjoy day dreams, but realise they can't eliminate past sorrow.

With a compass change of temper let's steer a calmer course tomorrow.

**Snow Change**

The car engine sat there smugly as if defying me to make further attempts at bringing it back to life, but knowing that

## Around the Buoys

by now the damned battery was flat I merely slammed the bonnet down spitefully, and stamped off through the boatyard door. Walking down the slipway feeling disgruntled, snowflakes again started to drift slowly past my eyes adding to the thick carpet underfoot that had fallen earlier that morning By the time I'd reached my canal boat "Marlin" they were sticking to my hair and the shoulders and sleeves of my jersey.

Once aboard I took stock of my situation, realising that I'd now have to walk the mile or so home to arrange for the car to be towed back to the garage. The only problem was, having driven up in the shelter and warmth of the vehicle, I wasn't now particularly well dressed for a "Scot of the Antarctic" trek home. However, I wasn't too concerned for I knew that in the lockers somewhere hung Sally's waterproof yacht survival plastic jacket and trousers, also, my sea boots were stuffed away somewhere under the bunk. To carry home some small engine parts for repair and the fruit and veg I'd bought en route, I decided to use a pillow case that needed laundering anyway.

As I rooted around for my requirements I still felt in low spirits and to be honest, I knew perfectly well the real reason for my despair, which truth to tell, had been nagging me, like a toothache for the past few weeks. Yes, I had to face up to it, and like it or not there was no escaping the fact that tonight was a "Party Night" and that was that, full stop.

Some folk dread facing spiders, some dread facing tigers, some fear the dentist, and I'm sure there's quite a few out there who hate the thoughts of nasty needle injections. But those sort of challenges I brush aside as small fry, of no consequence, until I enter a room or hall where a party is in full swing. Immediately I start to suffer from some sort of deep shock and paralysis, especially when dragged protesting to the dance floor by those cheerful ladies who are determined to humiliate you, insisting that every person in the world can dance.

My feet and legs refuse to cooperate and delight in becoming as stiff and as awkward as is possible. Then my arms join in by getting themselves into absurd positions and when my footwear unerringly covers quite a few innocent dainty shoes, the encouraging smiles that greeted my arrival on the dance floor change to becoming rather forced When I manage to sneak away at the first opportunity to a seat as far away as is possible, people seem quietly relieved and make no attempt to drag me back, leaving me to sit and mope on my own.

Lately, when at a party I've craftily learned to sit there with a fixed idiotic grin on my face banging the table and swinging my feet to the beat of the music, as though I'm having a whale of a time. Secretly, I keep glancing at my watch thinking *'Good! Another ten minutes have passed; it won't be long now before I can make a bolt for home!'*

Above the thundering din of the disco music most folk seem to talk normally and appear completely relaxed, but even though I shout and listen as best I can, I can't for the life of me make head nor tail of any conversation, or even think of anything clever or smart to say. Sally despairs of me and jokes I could make a lot of money becoming a professional 'wall flower' whatever that is, and seriously, we've both agreed that I'm far happier at a funeral than at a wedding or birthday celebration. My demeanour blends better into the background, she kindly explains, and it's been suggested 'You'd get more interesting small talk out of a tailors dummy,' which doesn't help matters.

So, as you can see, I wasn't in the best of moods as I pulled on the plastic trousers, then my black rubber boots and thick white seaboot socks, which I turned down over the top, sailor style. Suddenly I came up with a good idea. I could use one of the towels that also required laundering as a scarf and by wrapping it around my head and ears and tying it under my chin it would help to keep the cold out, smart thinking! I thought. The other towel I rolled up and stuffed into the elastic waistband, out of the way, but adding to my already stout figure.

Struggling into Sally's jacket and hood thing, was an effort and though normally too colourful for me, it would have to suffice, and made my ensemble more or less complete. This left only the pillowcase to fill with the odds and ends and I was ready for the snow trek home.

Trundling up the slipway, and out of the boat yard door, I passed my abandoned car and gave it a sly spiteful kick on the wheel, but in doing so I slipped on the now thick snow, nearly doing myself nasty injury. Again, this did nothing to improve my disposition, and I felt really 100% downhearted.

It was now nearly 11am, and I desperately tried to cheer myself by looking forward to arriving home by noon disregarding the snow underfoot and the burden of the pillow over my shoulder, which, although not a great weight soon caused my hands to become very cold. Fortunately, I discovered Sally's fur-lined white mitts in the pockets and with a mental 'Thank-You' to her, I soon forced them on.

On course for home now I neared a house where two tots were playing with their parents building a Snowman. As I approached, they spotted me and ran to the gate to greet me with smiles and waves, a little surprised, I cracked my face and did my best to smile back trying to look cheerful. Then, feeling a little guilty, I also waved and smiled to their parents who appeared to shout something back to me, but the scarf, or should I say towel, over my ears prevented me from hearing properly.

Progressing along the lane now with the snow easing a little, I noticed groups of girls and boys playing in the park across the way. They were having high jinks throwing snowballs and enjoying an icy slide where the path fell away slightly downhill. Again, I was little surprised but pleased when they ceased their activities and ran to the railings to smile and wave happily to me, forcing me to respond. This time I waved the sack in the air to them, causing great merriment and further waves of greetings.

Trudging on, I must confess I felt in a much better mood after seeing those cheery young faces and as if to improve matters further, a snow covered car drew up at the far kerb flashing

*Around the Buoys*

its lights and I could vaguely hear the horn being sounded. The two young passengers in the rear seats waved and pressed their noses to the window. The lady driver opened the door and shouted something I could only partially hear, but which sounded like "Have you lost your way again Dear?" Slightly puzzled, but thinking she was considering offering me a lift, I replied "No Thank you! I've had a breakdown and I'm going to arrange a tow." For whatever reason my response created a great deal of merriment, and with more horn blowing and waves they drove away.

Now you might think, like myself, I was receiving more waves and smiles than Princess Kate on her wedding day and when I crossed the canal bridge with two complete strangers giving me high fives, I put my mind to fathoming the reason for this over-friendliness. After some deep thought, I cleverly came up with what I was certain was the answer. During times of national stress when there is a common threat, such as wartime or a terrible disaster, even when we're all in the same boat with a power failure, or water shortage, people seem to be far more friendly and considerate. A more cheerful spirit seems to prevail. Now, with the heavy snowfall putting us all in the same pickle, hence, I reasoned, all this good humoured smiling and waving in my direction. Of course, I was right, I congratulated myself, for trundling along the main road where there were far more people afoot, I could see that most of them were smiling, nodding and shouting in my direction and it was obvious not all of them were friends of mine.

Quite happy now and pleased with my cleverness, I neared the road where I live, when a young Mum put the icing on the mornings cake by releasing her two wee kiddies allowing them to run to me with open arms. I was quite touched by this charming reception and the looks of happiness on their lovely faces. With two big hugs, and the suspicion of a tear welling in my eyes, we exchanged smiles and waved our happy "Bye-bye's." It suddenly struck me that after being in such low spirits a short time ago I was now in a better mood than I had been for years. All that happiness and those cheery smiles I'd encountered homeward bound had done the trick and changed my outlook completely.

Finally, I arrived at the entrance of the road where I lived and was suddenly surprised to catch a glimpse of my reflection in a full length mirror that stands in the butchers shop doorway. **I could hardly believe my eyes!!** For there facing me was a portly figure dressed in a snow speckled bright red jacket with hood attached, red leggings, black rubber knee boots with white woolly socks turned down. The matching white edged suede mitts contrasted with my face, which, especially my large bulbous nose, was red with the cold. The tasselled end of the white towel streamed out like a flowing beard and to cap it all, slung over my shoulder was a full sack with suspiciously exciting bulges in it! No wonder I'd had a pleasant walk home!

As I continued to stare in the mirror, a broad smile stole across the features of my reflection, for I knew now for certain I'd misheard what the lady driver with the car had shouted across to me. It hadn't been, "Have you lost your way again Dear?" But more likely, "Have you lost your sleigh and reindeer?"

Oh! My apologies. I should have told you earlier, it was **Christmas Day Morning**, and incidentally not only was I very popular at the Fancy dress party that evening, but also, most unusually, I thoroughly enjoyed myself as well, for my heavy rubber boots prevented me from being invited to grace the dance floor and my conversation was helpfully restricted to. **"Ho, Ho, Ho."**

**Carpet Baggers**

The ship's officers had invested in a number of large, expensive Bombay carpets to sell for a profit on their return home. However, changed orders diverted the vessel to New Zealand and sadly en route heavy weather had seen a spiteful wave penetrate down a forward untrimmed vent into the masthouse soaking the stored carpets. Weather improvement saw we sailors hauling them on deck and draping them over the dropped derricks to dry out, their bright pattern's giving the vessel a magical Indian Bazaar appearance. The men cheerfully suggested rigging them as sails to bolster our desperate 9 knots, but the Mate knocked, saying "I don't want to embarrass the Engineers!" Embarrassment still occurred when a passing smart-arsed US tanker morsed across, "Is your Limey bum-boat open for business?"

When dried the carpets were as good as new and the Officers decided to stow them aft in a lazarette where they would be safer weatherwise, which was sensible, but safer otherwise was questionable with the move being noted by the deck and engine room hands who also lived aft.

Arrival in NZ found the wary Master refusing a cash sub for the crew. This didn't exactly raise euphoria amongst the men, being alcohol free for some time, especially with an oasis called the "Waverly" beckoning seductively at the quays end. Personally, as well as the rotten prospect of losing sleep by being nominated as night watchman, things also didn't look good for my 21st birthday the next day, for my horizon predicted a distinct shortage of celebratory drinks.

Next afternoon, though, saw a great surprise when a brewer's dray parked alongside, with the eager 'deckies' swinging a yard arm and shipping its cargo of beer and whisky. Officers head-scratched as the drink was passed around with all hands invited to enjoy the occasion, no questions asked.

The alerted police showing wisdom that would have out Sherlocked Holmes soon discovered the carpets had disappeared, obviously to finance the operation and continuing their brilliant deductive powers decided to question the drunken crew. The men cordially invited the police to free drinks before eventually confessing to selling the carpets to certain stevedores. The crew's ring-leader and two dockers were quickly apprehended and taken to be held in what was rumoured to be 'custard' ashore. The carpets were retrieved and returned to the ship's officers.

The Captain refused to charge anybody being happy to retain his crew, the Police were happy getting their men, the Officers were happy getting their carpets back, the crew were happy getting their drinks, and even the stevedores, though admittedly not quite as happy, got a holiday with free haircuts. But I doubt if anybody was as happy as myself, for I got as drunk as a Lord, finishing up with a terrible hangover after the best 21$^{st}$ birthday party anyone ever had.

Confidentially, I didn't lose any sleep being night watchman, for I found the bunks quite comfy in the local Mt Eden prison before they bunged me back aboard when my vessel was ready to sail.

## Charlie Jones

I wonder, did you ever sail with 'shell back' Charlie Jones?

That's right, he signed as Bosuns mate and always made no bones

About the fact he loved his job, it's true, he loved the life.

(Of course he hid those feelings when on home leave with his wife)

A quiet man he never bragged nor wished for golden braid.

## Bill Backshall

He'd be too shy to march in a Remembrance Parade.

He 'got the hammer', (bought it twice) but he kept it to himself.

Just loved his home and Family said they really were his wealth.

On deck, he wore a paint splashed vest, even in the hottest sun

To hide his burns from a blazing tanker, sunk in '41.

He joked "I swam and did the crawl", (His style has us in tucks)

"I thought the back stroke in those flames might ruin my film star looks!"

Well old Charlie dragged his anchor; yes, he tacked across the Bar

Last port of call was Calabar (or did they bunker at Dakar?)

So his shipmates did the honours and they buried him at sea

With his little silver M N badge pinned where it ought to be.

No paparazzi cameras, for him no headline news

No television celebrity swag, (That stuff would blow his fuse).

A simple unsung seaman, and he'll be quite content to be

With some former Merchant shipmates, in the best of company.

**Cat Nap**

The Blue Star boat now loaded, was finally receiving prize cattle in prepared deck pens bound for S. America. A wooden cage was also ready on the boat deck for a valuable pedigree cat, but unfortunately, when transferring the frightened feline into its temporary home, it broke away and raced down the gangway disappearing in a flash. Worried stiff, the shore gang whose responsibility it was, sensibly retired to the nearest pub to discuss what to do about the accident. Luckily the Bosun spotted a scruffy, half-starved black cat creeping around the bar and though it was an unkempt mouser, he reckoned any cat was better than an empty cage. He grabbed it and unseen, managed to transport it back aboard where he stuffed it, after subduing some resistance, into the vacant cage.

The Mate, not having seen the original creature, shook his head doubtfully when viewing it, but reluctantly accepted, and placed it into the Stewardesses tender care. Being an animal lover, she lovingly groomed it, pampered it and fed it outward bound, and by the time it arrived at its destination, it suited the part and was accepted by the rich owner and lived happily ever after. The original pedigree cat is still happily roaming the Liverpool dock estate and lived happily ever after.

## Auntie'thesis

Some are destined to be fortunate, others to be unfortunate. Many years ago, my Aunt Ann enjoyed her life serving as a laundress/stewardess aboard various Cunard liners. The named photos of the "Samaria" and the "Laconia" as they hung in my Grandma's hall, registered in my child's mind, and at that stage it was my belief that Ann was second in importance only to the Captain.

She sailed around the world numerous times and by being a popular, cheerful, single and an attractive woman, with great daring, she gate- crashed first class evening dances and social events in the main saloons, meeting and mingling with the rich and the famous. My Aunt Jane's life was not quite as enjoyable.

Again in my developing child's mind, the word "Vestris", I overheard being mentioned by my adults in hushed conversation, was vaguely lodged somewhere in my memory locker, but I casually confused it with "Vesta's" which I had learnt were a popular make of matches, not a word I believed of any significance.

However, with the passing of time, I realised that the word actually referred to the S.S Vestris, a Liverpool passenger liner that had foundered in 1928 off the U S coast after listing in very stormy weather with a great loss of life. Amongst those who perished was the ship's baker, my Uncle Walter Chapman, Aunt Jane's husband. This tragedy left her to fend for herself, and raise her 5 year old son Walter in desperate circumstances, for she received no monies of any sort from any quarter for many, many long years, possibly due to prolonged legal marine liability argument, or indifference.

Through the late nineteen twenties/thirties, great privation was already being experienced nationally, for folk were extremely lucky to have employment, leaving Jane in a dreadful plight. She was forced to live in the bedroom of a rundown terrace house that flooded regularly up to ceiling height, permanently ruining the ground floor accommodation making it uninhabitable. This flooding was due to an inadequate sewage system for the whole area which unfortunately lay in a dell.

Scratching on the local tip for scraps of coal and wood to provide fuel for the tiny fire place was a regular embarrassing but necessary chore for Jane. The only lighting I witnessed on my visits was a small paraffin oil lamp that lit the sparsely furnished bedroom. Other forms of help were provided by her close family, though they themselves were experiencing harsh living conditions. Much later in life she received a pittance in compensation for her loss.

Despite this extreme adversity, Jane maintained a spirited sense of humour which was never quenched and then passed down to her son, Walter who, in later life would jokingly assure folk that as a child, "He grew up in the Lake District!!"

## Wild Goose Chase

"Wild Goose Chase"
(What sort of Vessel is This?")

The shipping clerk at the M.N, 'Pool' was rather annoyed, for I had refused to join a ship as a 'Junior' ordinary seaman, instead of my self-important 'Senior', O/S rating. So he engineered an unofficial wild goose chase to trim my vents. Smirking, he drew me aside and whispered, "Here you are then Son, you're on a 'Stand–by', Sunday morning. She's the 'Empire Mac Callum' lying at the Alexandra Dock. Take all the heavy weather gear you've got," he added spitefully. Knowing 'Fort' and 'Liberty' cargo boats, I assumed that

*Around the Buoys*

'Empire' boats would be much of a muchness. Well, so I thought.

The clerk's orders struck me as being unusual, normally 'Stand-by's' would hang around the 'Pool, or skulk around Paradise Street weekends waiting to be called should a vessel report in shorthanded. The last time I was on one, as I loitered by the deserted Sailors Home with my sea bag, a policeman gave me the old fish eye, but spotting my tiny M.N Badge, he scowled and frustratingly carried on pounding his beat.

On Sunday morn' telling my mother, "I may be away for months, or I may be home for tea," she looked resigned, for with two other seafaring sons, she now accepted hap-hazard comings and goings as normal confusion. With great fortitude I survived the rough overhead train ride to the Alex' Dock and lugging every stitch of my heavy weather clothing in a cumbersome case I enquired of a docker, "Where's the Empire Mac Callum berthed Mate?"

"That's her lying over there!" he pointed, but the vessel was obscured from view by the dockside warehouse. Entering the shed, I made my way to the gangway which was unusually poked through a gunport door in the ship's side, not straight onto the deck as is usual for a cargo ship. Lumping my damned case up the steep gangway, I climbed aboard blowing for tugs, only to be surprised, for my first impression was, "What the hell's this?"

I stood in a vast covered tween deck and wondered what I

was aboard. It was nothing like the average cargo vessel, no derricks, no masts, no winches, etc., just a dark grain dusty warehouse with lifeboats, tank tops, and clutter stuck all over the place. Spotting the Mate I reported to him and then enquired, "What sort of a vessel is this Chief?" Grinning, he informed me, "It's a Mac Ship, a Merchant Aircraft Carrier." Seeing my bewilderment he further explained, "She carries grain plus a few planes on top deck to protect the convoy." Then he took pity on me and smiled. "Somebody at the 'Pool is swinging your compass Son. We're not shorthanded so push off home and we'll try to cross the Atlantic without you!" I scuttled ashore as fast as I could, feeling relieved, for at that time I didn't like aeroplanes, they always wanted to drop nasty bombs on you.

Sixty years later, I saw a nostalgic wartime article in a newspaper which included a photo of the same 'Empire Mac Callum' at sea and for the first time I got a good look at that particular unusual carrier. Escorting her was a corvette. It looked like, and I hoped it was the H.M.S. "Wild Goose" one of Captain Johnny Walker's famous U-Boat chasers. Then, without telling fibs, I could boast to my wife, "I've been on both of those!"

**"Marlin". Voyage One**

As you well know, life can be sad, if not cruel at times, so it's nice to have someone around who can lighten things up by often romancing everyday circumstances.

Though saddled like the rest of us with an elementary school education, Spike was very intelligent, with a sense of humour which continually swamped being serious. Some situations eventually being transformed with light hearted acting or clowning. It was also contagious. His ambition had long been to be an actor and now, with our reluctant co-operation, here was his chance to perform and get some practice in. So just to humour him we mustered on the canal bank and lined up at the 'Attention' position, as you see soldiers do. Spike stepped up and balanced on an old engine block in front of us to emphasise his authority and looking down he loudly ordered, "Ships Company! At ease!" We tried to adopt the 'at ease' stance by moving legs apart, placing arms behind our backs and looking attentive.

"Now men," he began in a haughty, superior, Naval Officers tone, "Now men, we are joining a new vessel. A vessel we can all be proud of. A vessel which can help sweep the seas clear of the enemy." A vibrant pause, and then, scanning our faces, continued, "I know some of you have sailed under my command before," and here he picked out Eddie with a sweeping gesture, "You there Rankin! You were with me on my old destroyer H.M.S Hasty. Now I want you to tell your new shipmates what sort of fighting ship I want!" Eddie stepped forward and tried to salute smartly, "Yes Sir. A happy and efficient ship, Sir!"

"That's right my man," and dismissing Rankin back to the line, Spike carried on with his address. "But you can't have a happy ship without it being an efficient ship, nor an efficient ship without it being a happy ship." After this stirring advice and more lecturing about the 'Nelson Touch' and 'Searching out, attacking and destroying enemy warships', etc, all delivered in a very imperious tone, he then dismissed us with a nautical salute and a "Carry on and Good Luck!" He appeared well satisfied with his portrayal of Lord Louis Mountbatten addressing the assembled ships company about to board the newly commissioning destroyer H.M.S Kelly at a dreary wartime quayside. All of this as per the morale boosting, stiff upper lip, Royal Navy war movie 'In Which We Serve'. Spike's theatrics over, we returned to normality, and scrambled back aboard the "Marlin", an ex M V "Hinakura" twenty five foot steel lifeboat hull, which I'd bought at the Liverpool docks and having partly converted her, had now shoulder hauled her up the Leeds and Liverpool canal to a boat yard at Litherland.

I was really a simple 'wood, paint and putty man' who had reached the worrying stage of having to now provide the means of propulsion to what until now had been an engineless 'dumb craft'. Sadly, mechanics weren't exactly my strongest suit, but the old car engine I'd purchased cheaply had somehow been fitted and was coupled up to a very dodgy prop shaft which turned inside a lashed up home-made stern tube. This rig combined with a difficult gear change system had given me sleepless nights, but these fears I had kept hidden from the rest of the men.

"Right Bill," said Chay, "the engine's running sweetly now." Which was all very well, but finding the right gear was a matter of luck. However, after some experimenting and tinkering around, our choice was fortunate and suddenly things began to happen. To be honest a little too quickly for my liking. My heart leapt with excitement as the prop started to churn and the "Marlin" began to move forward, setting sail under her own power for the first time. Her maiden voyage had begun.

"Leggo fore and aft!" I shouted to Rankin on the bank as panicking, I flung myself to grab the tiller, but as he cast off the mooring lines the boat was now picking up way and he was left behind unable to jump aboard. The thought flashed through my mind that he didn't look too displeased, for he gave a grin, a wave, and pulling out a partly smoked 'ciggie' from behind his ear, bawled to me, "Don't worry Bill, I'll stand by the phone in the bar of the Jubilee pub should you need to ring me from Leeds or somewhere!"

Though I was dry mouthed with anxiety, I found the tiller was steering her quite well as she picked up her skirts and steamed North towards the nearby tannery. Being an A B, I felt confident that all was well in the deck department, but the engine room part with all that mechanical gubbins and nuts and bolts stuff was something else. However, my thoughts were broken by Spike, who was now on the little foredeck flemishing down the lines and occasionally gazing ahead with cupped hands over his eyes like the Ancient Mariner.

He now carried on practicing his extensive acting roles by bellowing to me, "I've sailed these waters before Skipper and I know every dangerous shoal and reef round here. Feel safe with me as your pilot." I knew he had laboured on the canal barges many years ago, but seeing we were only thirty yards or so from our moorings, this advice seemed a little unnecessary and alarmist, to say the least. Currie now questioned from the cabin, "Rankin's backed out Sir, shall I log him as Distressed British Seaman?"

"No," I retorted, "he's safe in the pub and far from being distressed." The "Marlin" was now sailing quite serenely so I relaxed a little and permitted the suggestion of a nervous smile to play around my lips but just then Chay and Spike joined me at the tiller. "Compliments of the crew Cap'n, but have you given any thoughts of how to stop this craft?" Chay questioned, and looking very serious Spike added, "We are

*Around the Buoys*

both married men with two chairs Sir, and we didn't come prepared for a long voyage."

"Courage men," I replied, steadying them whilst trying to mask my own concerns, for I suddenly realised I hadn't given the aspect of stopping much thought. "Please remember men, I've spent over the wrong side of fifty pounds and six months trying to get this craft under way, and as regards stopping her, I'm sure something will crop up to help us." Fortunately or unfortunately, the 'cropping up' happened right there and then, for the engine gave a couple of nasty sneezes, a cough or two, and finally cut out altogether. The "Marlin" drifted into the canal bank. Her maiden voyage was over.

Back at the boat yard by transferring the ballast forward, we put her down by the head and discovered the dodgy prop shaft had seized in the stern tube.

"Too good a fit!"

"Needs a thou or two off! And more lubrication," seemed the general consensus as they poked and prodded it with 'know it all' nods. So plans were made to whisk it back to the lathe for further attention. "Never mind tendering the work to Cammel Lairds!" spoke up Rankin, "Just leave it to me!" I felt he was hoping to atone for his skipping ship. But now came my pleasant surprise for the valiant crew. To celebrate the maiden trip, I now produced bottles of brown beer, tasty meat pies, and even a bottle of brown sauce from the forepeak where I'd cleverly hidden them. These refreshments went down well with all hands tucking in, for the danger and excitement of the trip had given us a good appetite. Unfortunately, as I selected a juicy pie, a passing boat owner's cry of "Ahoy Marlin!" distracted me, and looking away to answer him, I mistakenly selected a brown beer bottle for the sauce, and then inadvertently poured beer all over the pie and myself as well. Nobody laughed at my embarrassment, for they knew in their hearts I'd been through Hell and still got them back home safely to their loved ones.

Later on though, as we trundled up the slipway homeward bound with the offending shaft slung over my shoulder, I managed to overhear Spike whispering to the others in a theatrically aside voice, "Even though I can understand the pressure of command weighing heavily on our Skippers shoulders, I just couldn't see Lord Louis Mountbatten pouring ale over his meat pie."

**S.S John Holt**

**Bound for Apapa, Nigeria to view an unusual, Heavenly spectacle. Noon Time Stars**

## *Around the Buoys*

I would say about 60% of my brain cells were occupied with the business of painting the boat deck rails, and another 20% with chatting to my shipmates about the evening's football match with a nearby Swedish ship's team. Probably 10% were studying how long it would be before dinner time and what would be served up, with a further 5% warning me that my feet getting too hot and to get moving them into the shade. The other unoccupied 5% were sort of standing by, radar like; in case anything new occurred that my focusing brain might need to know about.

Eventually the 5% got the slightest suggestion of change. They weren't sure what it was, specifically, but kept alert waiting for something more definite. And it came. So they borrowed more and more attention from the other busy senses till they were strong and confident enough to notify my brain with the message "There's a change." The other senses now came to a casual stand-still joining in querying the new problem. Looking around I could see my shipmates were also beginning to become alert to some sort of change, so I definitely stopped the painting and other activities and concentrated upon the as yet unidentified alarm.

The normal day in Apapa, Nigeria, is one of tremendous heat and brilliant sunshine, and aboard the SS "John Holt", this particular day seemed no different, that is until a little before noon when my brain cells sensed something unusual. Slowly we vaguely began to notice that the blinding light of the midday sun seemed to be altering slightly to a softer, silvery caste as the minutes progressed.

Gradually the light continued to fail with the edges of shadows beginning to dissolve and as it was now just on noon we deck hands suddenly realised we had some sort of Sun/Moon eclipse taking place. There are no newspaper deliveries in Apapa and with the ships aerial being dismantled to facilitate cargo working, surprise was total. No forecast or even mention of any such happening had filtered down from the bridge and we doubted the officers themselves had any prior warning, for it was obvious it was going to be the whole hog, a total eclipse.

It grew steadily darker much to our interest, but not I'm afraid to our Kroo boys who worked the ship's cargo, nor to the Nigerian porters who found it more frightening than interesting and with the near onset of complete darkness they streamed up from the hatches and down the gangways to the apparent safety of the quayside warehouses where they huddled en masse shouting, "Night time now Boss! Go finish work now!" As far as they were concerned for some reason the day's work was over and it was now night-time.

Within a short space of time, darkness was absolute with stars appearing, twinkling merrily, a marvellous transformation from a red hot tropic day to a coal black night with the temperature falling rapidly. The vast harbour, usually noisy and bustling with activity at this hour, was now eerily quiet as people stood unbelieving as to what they were experiencing. Everything, reality, time, thought, and activity seemed unable to be judged. We were lost in a different time frame with folk tense, unthinkingly holding their breath, secretly praying for life to return to normality, anxiousness growing with every passing pitch black minute. Then, but even then just noticeably, things started to creep back to normal minute by minute, with our ordinary daylight returning to us, relaxing nerves and muscles.

Now from the bridge officers to the engine room staff, from the catering men to the deck hands, nervous conversation returned, rather forced and garbled as if to cover vague feelings of hidden anxiety. The natives were reluctantly returning from the sheds ill at ease, for it had been a terrifying incident for them, and quite alarming to ourselves if the truth be told, until we had realised what was occurring and even then, deep down a primitive fear lurked hidden below the surface of our minds. It really was an awe inspiring occasion, adding another of those seafaring unforgettable memories to store away for a lifetime.

With the return of daylight, things soon assumed normality and people appeared quite animated and light hearted, discussing the unusual event, but with a hint of hidden nervousness, as people often do after an embarrassing experience. Later, I couldn't help but think of the people who lived tens of thousands of years ago and what their thoughts must have been when faced with a similar event.

One solution would have been to have appeased the angry Gods of the time with a sacrifice or two, and as our ship days later steamed up the narrow jungle creeks of the Niger Delta, at certain holy places, on stilts in shallow water at the bank side, small wooden covered platforms could be seen where food and other valuable offerings are left regularly to placate their Juju Gods. Noticing my amused, slightly cynical interest viewing them, a Kroo friend "Pepper Soup" suggested, in what sounded like a remindful and correcting tone, "All same churches for Liverepools, Massah Bill! When Fear first Walked the Earth, Gods were Born." A saying came to mind, but from I know not where.

**The Old Shellback**

He called in a pub and encouraged by drink

He let loose his tongue, (but neglected to think).

For gathered around sat our present day youth.

Well, they listened at first, but they soon grew uncouth.

For you know how it is when we old seamen spout.

We were ill rigged and hungry and never had 'nout'.

How we paid off with washers, then we'd probably brag

About dodging the 'tin fish' and all that old swag.

Well, they teased and derided him for "Blowing his Horn"

Till he stamped home disgruntled feeling rather forlorn.

But later that night as he thought "Who's to blame?'.

He examined his own youth, and head shook with shame.

*Around the Buoys*

To be perfectly honest, he'll admit under stress

When he was their age, he hates to confess

He too used to laugh at his elders, it's true.

He was to full of himself to pay them their due.

If he'd have been smarter, he'd have smiled at their jeers.

For when you grow old you can judge how the years

Steal away, whilst the young take their eyes off the ball

And mock us, not knowing it comes to us all.

**Clinging to the Wreckage**

Yes I know this report seems farfetched, well of course it is, for most of the story's content comes from the South Pacific and you can't fetch anything further than that. Still, I'll concede it was a strange business all round, part truth, part history, part geography, and part a good percentage of my bloody imagination. Trim your vents on the wind and I'll tell you how it all came about.

As usual between voyages, I enjoyed the never ending task of converting into a cabin cruiser my ex "Hinakura" steel lifeboat now moored on a canal, and once again I had the bright idea to change my boat's name from "Marlin" to "Papeete". This was mainly because I'd fallen in love with the picturesque harbour of that name on the island of Tahiti during earlier seafaring days whilst aboard a vessel tramping around the South Pacific.

The idea of a name change for the boat had been irritating, or should that be germinating, in my mind for quite a long time, like a wee pearl does in an oyster or wherever the hell it is they grow. I believed the name would suit my craft better, more interesting and mysterious, then folk would hopefully enquire, "Where the hells that place Bill?" Or, "How did you arrive at that strange name?" and I could then swing the lamp, and blow about some well-rehearsed seafaring yarns, starting with, "When I was sailing around the Polynesian Islands." So, do it I did.

I unscrewed the old name plates off the bows and temporary painted the new name on two small pieces of wood, screwed them back in situ, rang the Waterways clerk about the change of name and hey-ho, the switch was done. But gradually, I began to realise that ever since changing the name, I'd had an unbelievable run of misfortune, sad bereavements, silly accidents, saying the wrong things to folk, a run of poor health, losing cash, faults with the boat engine, car problems, all sorts of negative things, and after quite a lot of careful thought discounting various more obvious reasons, I finally wondered if it had anything to do with a curious incident that happened during my last visit to Tahiti some years ago, but still vivid in my memory.

Surely not, it couldn't possibly be I thought, however I selected full astern in my memory locker and examined the incident over and over again in my mind, just to see if it could in any way have any influence or connection, though really it did seem rather tenuous.

We had arrived at the beautiful magic island of Tahiti aboard a tramp steamer whilst on the phosphate run around the South Pacific. Seafarers will probably know the triangle trip, Nauru or Makatea to load phosphate, then across to Aussie to discharge, thence back to New Zealand to load part cargo for the Society and Cook islands and so on back to Makatea, etc.

This run regularly entailed crossing that damned International Date Line, skipping a complete day one way, and having two days repeated the other way. All very confusing, till the Mate decided we should work just half a day whenever transiting occurred, leaving we deck hands trying to look happily contented but secretly completely confused. Well, at least we didn't have to think things out anymore, but God knows if we won or lost on the deal.

Anyway, it happened to be a Sunday morning when we berthed at the island in question on this particular trip, and 'Windy' Miles and I went ashore for a little 'rubber necking,' as the Yanks call it. We enjoyed visiting the open air market, the quaint waterfront with the famous Quinn's bar, the broad smiles of the friendly folk, and the perfect weather etc.

Later, a little further afield we stumbled upon a small white painted museum, Windy reckoning it was attributed to the

French artist Paul Gaughin who, he announced with his know-all smirk, after falling in love with the place and the wahines there, painted a lot of colourful stuff and then 'Dragged his anchor with a dose of syph'. Just another of Windy's descriptive pearls of wisdom. I accepted and understood his description, but for strangers to seafarers terms, and to put it more politely, he died of 'love sickness', as the Tahitians call it. In the museum grounds wandered a large old turtle about the size of a small car, which we learnt with a certain degree of doubt, was supposed to have been alive when the "Bounty" berthed there.

Lying on the lawn on display, was a large badly weathered Admiralty pattern anchor, which our guide spent time trying to assure us, originally belonged to the H.M.S Bounty itself, leaving us again with cynical raised eyebrows, but also prompting us to accept and concede this was in fact the scene of the notorious Mutiny.

Also of interest some yards away stood a seven foot high stone statue of the Pacific island's God called "Tiki." The guide told us that his people, the Polynesians, still fervently believed their God to be alive and very powerful, and he whispered to warn us very seriously with wide open eyes, that to mock, or touch it would bring a bad luck curse.

Naturally, being a young, disbelieving, disrespectful Liverpool lad, as well as being a smart arse, I immediately sniggered and smacked it on its backside a few times bellowing "Hiya, Tik, how yer blowin' it whacker?!" causing the guide to appear desperately concerned, for he immediately warned us that to lift the curse now cast upon me, it was believed I would have to 'Free Spirits!', whatever the hell that meant. "These beliefs and supposed curses are just cooked up local legends to frighten and intrigue the tourists!" scoffed Windy, and I agreed as we dismissed his remarks as rubbish.

Time passed by without either of us giving any further thought to the matter and later on after completing the long voyage, we drifted apart joining different vessels. A lot of nothing much happened in that direction for a year or two as I got a couple of voyages under my belt until, as I was initially telling you, I changed the name of my little canal boat from "Marlin" to "Papeete" and, to repeat, from then on things seemed to drift towards continual misfortune and downright bad luck. However, after negating studied thought of other reasons that maybe causing the down period, I remembered, but just couldn't believe it had anything to do with that silly "Tiki" episode with its enigmatic curse.

So I dismissed the whole Pacific thing as a non-starter and concentrated upon trying to fix the damned engine and stern tube problems. I was in no hurry for I could sleep aboard, seeing my boat was moored in the "Rock Cutting" a nice sheltered countryside spot with a high, roughly hewn sandstone wall one side and a slow rising tree lined bank on the other. This stretch was steeped in history, for it was where the canal diggers, mainly Irish "Navies" had forced their way through sandstone rock for hundreds of yards when starting to excavate the local section of the Leeds & Liverpool canal, all those donkeys years ago. Once through that tremendously difficult natural hazard, a feat comparable in effort to a miniature Culebra Cut, the rest would be still be terribly hard work, but at least straight forward on to Liverpool through flattish agricultural land.

With night drawing on, after struggling with the repairs and the leaking stern tube, I had a cuppa, and wearily climbed into the bunk soon to enter the land of nod, absolutely out to the world. Sometime later though, I partly wakened to notice although it was a full moon. It was an unusually misty moonlit night outboard, but then I disappeared back to sleep. Only to awaken again shortly after, and in a sec' fall asleep again, until I wasn't sure if I was conscious or not. It was during this confusing period I became aware of the sound of oars being quietly used, or something that sounded dammed like them, a regular splashing, plopping sound with squeak of rusty rowlocks.

Curious, I crawled out of the bunk and peeped through the forrad window. I was shocked and frankly frightened to see what appeared to be the ghostly spirits of ancient bearded mariners in an old whaler drifting along in the misty moonlight being rowed by one man whilst the five or six scruffily dressed others lay slumped over their oars. Before the moon became obscured causing a darker scene, I could see in the stern sheets an Officer at the tiller dressed in old tattered Admiralty regalia uniform, apparently attempting to scrutinise the name on the bows of my boat as they drifted near. But the fading light and the smallness of my painted name letters obviously defeated him, for I could see him plainly shaking his head negatively to the other boat members. However, it didn't defeat my efforts at recognition, for I could clearly read the name on the transom of the cutter, which was inscribed in large old English lettering. It spelt the name "Bounty".

As they passed away out of sight, I groggily returned to my bunk and within a few minutes was drifting to sleep again, unsure whether I'd actually seen, or dreamt the episode, common sense making me more or less lean towards the latter. Yes of course it must have been a dream, but then I recalled, dreams are generally vague, mostly hard to remember, and seldom make sense, changing from one thing to another, yet this one seemed to be quite believable with clarity and continuity.

The next day found me in my local library searching for any information that was available about the Mutiny aboard that unhappy ship the "Bounty", for my dream, or whatever it was, had me intrigued and curious about any facts I could dig up. I was a little embarrassed too, for wasn't I the one who for years had pooh-poohed all talk of ghosts, flying saucers, fortune tellers, spiritualists etc and yet here I was researching a ghostly whaler and the spirits of men from all those years ago, so whilst browsing through the books, I sensibly decided to keep this embarrassing business to myself, I didn't fancy being laughed at.

After a long search I found an interesting book upon the Society Islands group, where Tahiti is the main island and in a small chapter devoted to the subject I stumbled upon certain coincidences that in my imagination might well have acted as a magnet to attract any ghostly spirits still adrift from that troubled vessel I found a quiet corner and sitting there gathering my thoughts, reviewing where I was at, with this unusual business.

Firstly, I had visited Papeete the port of Tahiti a few times myself, secondly, my small boat, which was now named after that harbour, had also visited there regularly, for it had been a lifeboat aboard the cargo liner "Hinakura" calling regularly to the port en route for New Zealand. Also in my possession was my prized polished wooden cigarette box holder, formed in the shape of a turtle with a beautiful coloured Sea Shell as a lid.

Then again, I found it was exactly 200 hundred years ago since the Mutiny, 1789. I had researched earlier and found that though the first ceremonious sod for the canal was dug 1777, a few years later it was in 1789 when they commenced to dig the stretch of canal, the 'Rock Cutting,' where I was moored and had that dream thing. Very strange and coincidental indeed, the two incidents occurring simultaneously. Reading my book further, I was surprised to find that not one, but two whalers had been cast adrift by the mutineers, with one boat, under Captain Bligh after a tremendous feat of seamanship, arriving at Dutch East Timor, from where they were transported safely back to England.

The other cutter was cast adrift later and obviously wasn't as important to history, therefore it was hardly documented and as a matter of fact, never heard of again. This latter knowledge left me wondering whimsically was that particular boat and its crew still adrift on the Sea of Time, continually searching for their beloved harbour, and by some time warp exchange of contemporary incidents confused over their whereabouts and now mistakenly haunting the 'Rock Cutting' looking for their safe haven of Papeete?

I read, but already knew, of the popular myth that having visited the island once, a person will be bound to return again someday, and having viewed the Bounty's anchor will never be free, forever hooked to the harbour. Were the missing crew captivated by this supposed myth, but searching the wrong zone? A rather contrived explanation I accepted, criticising myself, but still the whole thing was a mix up.

Anyway, about that myth of being compelled to return to the island someday. Who the hell would want to disagree with that belief? Bravely, I decided to revisit the 'Rock Cutting' again whilst the Moon was still pretty full, and spend another night there, mainly to see if anything further transpired in my dream or in actuality. Only this time I took a bottle of whisky, purely as a night-cap, I kidded myself, but truthfully, I was nervous about the ghostly apparitions that may occur and thought a tot or two would bolster my courage.

Following my previous routine, I arrived there at the same time, pottered around, made a meal, and read that library book whilst having a tot or two, then I decided to turn in, but just before switching the little bunk light off, my eyes fell upon my favourite curio, that carved cigarette holder in the shape of a turtle made from a lovely polished piece of wood, with a most beautiful sox inch sea shell lid, the only prized memento I had in my possession from Tahiti. Cursing, I realised that it was a mistake admiring it, for it would probably lodge in my brain whilst I slept and maybe influence my dreams.

Again, I slept well until early morning, when I started to awaken, then drift back to sleep, only to come to again, until I was suspended between semi-consciousness and uncertainty, just as the other night. But then with a nervous shiver and with the hairs on the back of my neck performing a little dance, I began to hear the same sounds of oars being quietly used, causing me to crawl out of my bunk apprehensively, and peep through the forrad window.

With my heart pumping madly I realised I wasn't the bravest man in the world, for I could see the moonlight was much brighter this time, giving me a clearer view of the ghostly cutter outlined against the water edged trees on the far bank, and yes I could plainly see the Officer at the tiller still scanning keenly ahead. This time, though, with the brighter moonlight I could see he managed to read the name "Papeete" on the bows of my craft. I could see the excitement he created as he aroused the exhausted seamen, for within seconds they were all agog waving and gesticulating and though it was a little difficult to hear anything properly with the hullabaloo, I could somehow sense what it was they were shouting, "Papeete! Papeete! Safe Haven, Papeete, Safe Haven!!" and immediately they

## Around the Buoys

commenced rowing vigorously towards the bows of my craft. Picking up speed, their cutter then hit the area where the name plate of the boat was and with a crashing "Thump!!" caused her to lurch and at the same instant I was startled to find I'd just fallen out of my bunk and was now lying on the hard deck breathless and confused!

Motionless for a minute or two, but properly awake now, I realised that after the excitement it had probably all been a vivid dream, with the fall awakening me. Well what an anti-climax, what a let-down, I grimaced as I climbed back into my bunk after checking all was peaceful outboard, but laying there thinking about the whole curious business, I began to be aware I was filled with a strong feeling of peaceful tranquillity, as if a great weight had been lifted from my shoulders making me feel I hadn't a care in the world. I hadn't felt so relaxed for some time, causing me to sleep the sleep of the innocent.

The next morning I arose full of the joys of spring, again feeling better than I had for months and I knew things were beginning to pick up positively, for my breakfast toast didn't burn and fall on the deck butter side down. I didn't need the toilet roll to staunch the blood from the morning shaving cuts that I generally suffer, and most unusually, the engine fired and started on the first attempt and then ran like a sewing machine, sounding in good nick. Even the stern tube hadn't leaked overnight, meaning I didn't have the labouring nuisance of bailing her out, thank goodness. Yessiree things were improving and I could sense my run of ill fortune was over. The tide of bad luck was ebbing fast and good stuff flooding in. As I stood in the open wheel house enjoying the sweet early morning country fresh air, I became aware one little thing was spoiling my happiness and I realised it was the acrid smell from the whisky bottle I'd had a tot or two from the night before. Twisting my face in dislike, for I simply can't stand the smell of the stuff during daytime, so, finding it repugnant I grabbed it, and seeing there wasn't a great deal left, I poured the remains over the boat's side into the canal. As the contents touched the water, it immediately spread out in multi colours dispersing as if it was happy to have been liberated, and then I gave the bottle a passage too.

At that precise second, it seemed a bolt of lightning struck me. I gave a great bellowing shout of 'Yeah!' For I now understood, and punched the air with my fist. I had the answer to it all, and didn't some guy shout "Eureka!" at a like moment. Last night by some peculiar dreamlike means, I'd hopefully liberated a number of ghostly 'Spirits' from their eternal wandering captivity, and now this morning I'd again freed another 'Spirit' from its captivity into the water. I wondered now if the Pacific god "Tiki" looked a little less stony faced at the moment in that Museum Garden of Papeete, having now, I hoped and believed, forgiven me and lifted his bad luck curse. I'm sure he must have known that I'd completed my penance by "Freeing Spirits" as advised by the museum guide of long ago.

Thinking things over, like quite a lot of folk I still don't believe in all that mumbo-jumbo, ghostly spirit stuff. However, between you and me, just to be on the safe side, (but much to the annoyance of the clerk in the Waterways Registration Dept). I quickly cancelled the change of my boat's name, and reverted it back from "Papeete" to good old "Marlin" again.

Actually, I thought twice about reporting this little snippet, but when changing the little name plates once more, I found the one on the starboard bow hanging on by a screw as if it had been struck by something. No comment. As yet I have no plans to comply with that myth about being obliged to visit Tahiti again. But if I do, I might just pat that "Tiki's" head very gently, and then whisper a word or two of contrition in his ear. Then again, maybe not.

**Twin Screw**

Previous to 'B.C.' (Before Containers) you could say it began at the top of Fort Road opposite the popular "Caradoc" pub. Then it swung south along Regent Road carrying on past the vast Stanley warehouse, crossing the busy Pier Head with its imposing office buildings, then on through, at that time, a more dreary area to pick up Sefton Street where it eventually came to an end at the Herculaneum, or was it the Herculuvian Dock. I honestly don't think many dock workers were quite sure how to pronounce it, let alone spell it, but solving things by calling it the "Herky".

I'm talking about 'Down the Dox' where a large proportion of the male population living in local terrace houses of Liverpool were employed. Yes, I'm talking about down the Docks. Seven miles of shipping berths, massive dock sheds, busy jam packed quays, disused wharfs, blitzed jetties, canyon like dry docks, nooks and crannies with cargoes strewn around awaiting transportation to every major port or backwater in the world. Boston or Bombay, Freetown or Fremantle, Genoa or Geelong, or every city, town and village in our Kingdom.

Timber, cotton, ground nuts, rubber, vehicles, wet hides, bicycle bells, all manner of imports, and exports, just come up with something and somewhere along the line, someone would be loading, pushing, stowing, trucking, slinging, or maybe even illegally breaking a wooden crate open to inspect it. That somebody would be one of the thousands of workers served either on the dock estate or in the mean side streets to the East of the 'Dockers Umbrella'. O.K I'm sure you know of the overhead railway that once was, but now, sadly, like a high proportion of the dockland installations, it is now just a hazy memory to some grey haired ex dock workers.

Stevedores, seamen, ship repair men, scalers, fruit porters, lady cleaners  timber skins, all manner of tradesmen , all mixed together like liquorice allsorts, thousands of souls all breathing, pushing and shoving, coming and going, some to labour locally, others to board vessels taking them to the extremes of the  Earth and without so much as a head turn, let alone a wave of 'Goodbye' from the indifferent blasé stevedores who heaved, strived, swore and  guided boxes, crates and sacks etc to their positions ready for trans

## Around the Buoys

locating. A giant mixing pot of men. Hard and lazy workers, honest and dishonest, some indifferent, some conscientious, ambitious and downcast, optimistic men and miserable sods. Where you could meet all the commodities of mankind, there also could you meet all the characteristics of mankind. Men who simply worked there and were going to work there, as long as the work was available. Individuals who dreamed of doing better in life, but only dreamed. Men who were determined to break free from the dockland and probably would, but with what success remained to be seen. Men who had broken free but had returned, too ill equipped to make the grade east of the dockland. Blow-bags who were going to make a million but only with their mouths of course, and quite few who didn't even bother to think or make plans, but just aimed at the next limited few hours ahead, concerned only with spending whatever cash was at their disposal in the pub or betting shop. Most of these men having received the most elementary education, and had suffered an extremely long and hazardous war, now faced only labouring work, if they were lucky.

Now and again you may run up against a man who appeared to be a little different. A man who seemed to be swimming against the tide of things, just a little better dressed than most guys, probably a non-smoker who didn't seem to drink as much alcohol as his mates. A quieter man, who didn't swear as profanely as you come to expect along the line. A man who didn't rely too much on Lady Luck like the ordinary punters sitting in the canteen studying the 'Nags', but a man who was determined to create his own good fortune, slowly it's true, but then again, the 'Dox' weren't built in a day.

This type of person was inspected with lowered eyebrows and written off as someone outside of what was expected. Bracketed with the religious fanatics and the up country 'Wooly-Backs', if you didn't conform to the ordinary guys, and talk the talk, you were some sort of a 'Phoney!'

Against this background Martin and his brother Pat O'Neil stood out in my mind as a pair prepared to swim against the current, but they knew the time wasn't right just yet. Jobs were scarce so we kept within the perimeter of the dock estate where jobs, even though poorly paid, were at least available to those of us who knew the ropes and where the 'stands' were to get 'taken on'.

The three of us got to be close friends whilst working for a small gig-boat firm that tended to the ships moorings. Just three of us perched on an empty quay in midwinter waiting for a vessel to berth, should give a clue as to why it was known as 'gulling.'

I took to the brothers at once especially Martin, for he and I hit off right away with the same outlook and interests in things. Just sitting on the bitts looking at the ships, we didn't need to talk too much, like you feel obliged to with some folk and I gathered that he seemed determined to carry out his plans of betterment for the future. "Just waiting for the break Bill", he assured me, "And I'll be 'Hoffman 'just as fast as my little clothes pegs will take me!" In a way it was like

*Around the Buoys*

planning and waiting for a gaol break that you see on the movies.

We worked the line of Docks for a while but it was inevitable that we would split at some stage, and when we did meet, it was an occasion for a cuppa' and a tab nab over a lot of excited conversation, for there was expectation that major car plants were moving into the area bringing prosperity and I could sense that Martin was getting itchy feet ready for his "Hoffman" to a better and more interesting job.

After that last meeting there was a complete lack of sightings for some months, until late one afternoon when the Holt boat I was working aboard let go her back spring as we shifted ship to Birkenhead. Twenty foot clear of the quay I pulled the fender aboard and at the same time I heard a loud voice hail me, "Now Bill!! How's it goin!?" It was Pat O Neil waving strongly from the back of a painter's lorry. "Hello Pat!" I returned, delighted to see him. "We're just in time to be too late for a gab together!" and we exchanged broad smiles as we realised there wasn't time for any lengthy discussions, for as my vessel pulled away from its mooring, his lorry was beginning to draw away up the quayside.

Cupping his hands to his mouth, he shouted "Keeping alright?"

"Not too bad Pat, though between you and me, I've had to spend time up in Walton I've been out of the game for a few months, that's why you haven't seen me lately." It was too late to go into details about my ulcer operation and convalescence.

The distance between us was now increasing rapidly, so with one last effort I bellowed, "How's my mate Martin?" Pat's tone seemed to change as he shouted back, "Didn't you hear about him? He's finished up in Winnick Mental Hospital, but he's doing alright!"

"In Winnick?" I screamed, unbelievably. But it was too late now for any further exchanges so I just stood there dumbfounded. *'Jeez I can't believe that'* I told myself over and over again. But there it was, I'd heard it with my own ears and even though it was a good distance there was no mistaking what Pat had shouted. Martin in a Mental hospital. I just couldn't take it in. All day as I was going about my work I mulled over the fact that my best pal, who always seemed so cool, calm, and collected was now suffering from this dreadful breakdown.

I regretted now not making stronger attempts at keeping in touch, but it was too late now for those sort of feelings. Eventually I found out where the O'Neil family lived and made arrangements to visit Pat one evening. He answered the door when I finally identified the correct terrace house. "Hello Bill! What a pleasant surprise to see you standing there." His face wreathed in smiles as he greeted me by shaking my hand vigorously, "Come on in!"

He invited me, leading me into the pleasant living room. After the usual compliments and again repeating his surprise, he asked me what he could do for me. "Well, Pat," I replied, "I thought I'd call to get the facts about Martin's breakdown, see if there's any improvement, and maybe get his address and the Ward number in Winnick. Maybe I could visit him at the weekend." Pat sat down facing me and his face was a picture to behold with a mixture of changing emotions altering his craggy features. Puzzlement finally being the winner as he asked me, "What bloody breakdown Bill?"

"Why Martin's breakdown, of course. You remember what you shouted to me the last time we met when I was on that Holt boat, you said he was in Winnick Mental Hospital. I never dreamed he'd suffer from stress like that, but at least he'll get good treatment there." Pat returned my gaze for a long drawn out ten seconds with the look puzzlement slowly turning to realisation dawning upon his face. "No! You bloody crackpot!" he burst out. "You've misunderstood me. He's not in there as a patient for crying out loud. He got a job there as an auxiliary nurse and now he's studying for that S R N thing, whatever they call it. Jeez that's the best joke I've heard for a long while." Pat was now doubled up in bulk, laughing uncontrollably, "Wait till I tell Martin about this one."

I could, of course, now see the funny side of it myself as I joined in the laughter, realising all my worrying had been a waste of time caused by a silly misunderstanding. Finally, we settled down and as Pat volunteered to make a cup of tea, we returned to yarning about the 'Old days'.

Pausing for a while in his conversation, I could see Pat was thinking about something else and with a little throat clearing I judged he was about to spit it out. "Look Bill, I don't want to pry into your business, or seem too nosey, and if you'd rather not tell me that's OK. But to be honest Martin and I were very concerned when you told me you'd been in Walton for a few months. What the hell went wrong? Did you get caught by the police with some swag going out of the Dock gate? Or something like that?

"Mart said it couldn't have been anything serious as you're not a guy like that. Anyway with you being a first offender with time off for good behaviour, you probably only did six or seven weeks. What the hell happened?" It was my turn to appear absolutely mystified. "What the hell d'you mean time off for good behaviour?" But now even as I spoke, my penny of realisation dropped. "No you fool; I wasn't in Walton Gaol for some bloody crime. I was weeks in Walton Hospital for an ulcer operation and off work for recuperation."

"Chrise! What a laugh, did you think I was in the big house for a stretch? Honest to God, you're as thick as me at misunderstanding things." Shaking off tears of laughter again, Pat said, "Naturally, when you said you were in Walton for a spell I thought you'd been awarded three penn'orth by some Judge," and again we collapsed in bulk, shaking our heads at our stupidity.

Saying our Goodbyes, we promised to meet again regularly, as you do, but of course we soon slipped back into the old routine of going our own ways without much contact. I

*Around the Buoys*

eventually followed in Martin's footsteps and did a "Hoffman" myself getting work away from the 'Dox', and this meant repairing, and selling small properties. At first it wasn't very profitable nor successful, for I followed my father's guidance being completely honest in my dealings. But foolishly to make a quick profit I started to employ illegal cheap labour, use inferior materials, 'cook the books' as they say, and carry out various other smart alec fiddles, which I won't go into details over. Naturally, I was worried, but I planned in time when in a better position, to go honest like most firms eventually do, and hoist the flag of respectability.

A year on I was viewing a property near the dock estate when I ran into Pat O'Neil and after exchanging greetings, I enquired about my old pal Martin. His face saddened a little. "Didn't you hear about Mart?" "No," I replied, getting the feeling I'd heard that remark before. He paused for a second. "Well, it seems the studying and pressure of the Nursing exams, coupled with his depressing divorce problems, were too much for him, and sadly he had a nervous breakdown. He's been in Fazakerly Psychiatric Ward for some time now, but with a bit of luck he should be home shortly; It's a heart break isn't it?"So, unusually, the two silly misunderstandings from years ago came in time, to be true. Martin did finally end up as a patient in a mental ward, and I'd best hurry to finish this account for the lights go out pretty early here in Walton Goal.

*Bill Backshall*

**"But Didn't You Know?"**
**"Black Morgan"**

He was a peculiar Bosun to say the least, even to find aboard a tramp steamer, and even that's something of an understatement. Ill kempt, aggressive, erratic, bad tempered, bothered, unpredictable, he easily qualified for the category that is known amongst seamen as a 'Headcase'. His party showpiece was to eat paper, match sticks, partly smoked lit cigarette ends, etc., though I imagine this was mainly to attract attention. He was nicknamed "Black Morgan" by the cheery Liverpool crew mainly because of his habit of helping to conserve the world's supply of soap and also because of his black beard and swarthy complexion. On the hottest of tropical days when all the deck hands were singled up in shorts and sandals, he continually wore the same old khaki shirt and slacks.

The sailors were a little wary of his aggression at the start of the trip, until he threw a piece of cotton waste at a tough young A B who soon squared up and put him on the deck. From that moment on he was reduced to being a figure of ridicule, but at the same time he became more friendly and accepted. I, personally, with most of the other men, lost my respect for him and in my youthful mind; he was just a crackpot who didn't know what day it was.

One steaming hot day in the Red Sea the Mate gave me a work log to pass to the Bosun. I knocked on his cabin door and was told to "Come in." For the first time I saw him with his shirt off, leaving his back exposed, and I was horrified by to see a mass of repulsive ugly scars and weal's that disfigured his back and upper arms. Every inch of his skin was in a dreadful condition and as I gawped, he turned and thanked me for my efforts without apparently noticing or being aware of my revulsion. "But didn't you know Bill?" replied Taffy, a quiet Welsh A B, as I told him of my surprising discovery, "Oh yes, Black Morgan was on an oil tanker during the war which got itself torpedoed and the poor sod said he was doing well in the water until the bloody floating fuel oil got ablaze. He told me he nearly got frazzled and just kept on ducking his head under water, letting his back get burned rather than his face. He always joked he didn't want to lose his film star looks.

"Eventually he was picked up by two shipmates in a life boat and he lay in agony, soaking his back in the salt water in the bilges for two days. He always reckons that's what turned him into a bloody loon!" *'Well'*, I thought, *'the poor sod, he's got good reason to be a little bit cracked'* and maybe I should have given him a little more leeway, but truth to tell, I don't think he expected any sort of feelings or sympathy like that, from people like me.

**Teddy Wilson**

He certainly wasn't the most attractive man on earth, small of stature, hardly a pick on him, with bones more in evidence than flesh. Bad enough you might think, but his eyes were the features that most impressed me. Not only were they well set back into their sockets but they were emphasised by the extraordinary bags that hung under them.

Apart from these things, Teddy was a nice, very quiet, pleasant sort of guy. In fact, to be honest, he was too quiet and inoffensive to the extreme, even when I'd make clever arsed remarks about his well lived in face and its accessories, he'd never respond with any great show of spirit. Just a slow smile.

During the days banter my references alluded to suggesting that he curbed his fast living lifestyle, cut out the drinking, smoking, womanising etc., but my joking leg-pulls only made Teddy smile further and then he would quietly join in the fun of the moment and that's all he would commit himself to. Once I suggested I'd win a beauty contest between the two of us, "Only just," was his gentle reply, "for you're no oil painting yourself Willie boy!" And though it was a fact, I was surprised he retaliated at all, let alone in such a cheerful and light hearted way.

He never spoke of his family life, probably because I never enquired about it. I suppose I was too full of myself to take any real interest in his background, concerned with my own important affairs, probably like the rest of the shore gang. So there he was then, just a quiet nice guy who resisted getting shirty no matter what leg pulling he got. Actually, I liked him more than I thought, admired him really. The only trouble was I never thought about it. It was as simple as that.

## Around the Buoys

Teddy eventually took a driving job to have more time with his young family, the shore gang employment calling for difficult hours away from home. So it was all the more of a terrible shock when we heard the dreadful news that Teddy had been killed in a tragic accident at the docks. Eventually we found that whilst loading his vehicle at the South Gladstone with a cargo of large Latex rubber bales, sadly one fell from the high sling and landed upon our friend, causing death immediately. We could only hope and pray he probably didn't know what happened.

I seem to recall hearing this remark before when Sammy, Teddy's brother in law, told me, "But didn't you know Bill? He was taken prisoner early in the war, when his vessel was sunk by a German armed raider and unfortunately he finished up in a hellish slave labour camp in East Germany, where he damn near starved to death for years. The prisoners there didn't even get the normal provisions and contacts that most POWs got in normal camps. Just fancy after years of near starvation and privation he finally got home for a spell and now this. What a sad end to a life."

Well, I thought, the poor man had good reason to be of such an appearance and so withdrawn. Maybe I should have given him a little more leeway, but Teddy didn't expect anything like that from people like me.

Maybe I should have learned a lesson from Black Morgan.

## Mrs Dinton

I finally decided to give the dockland life a rest, feeling I wanted a change, so with my few pounds savings burning a hole in my sky, I became self-employed repairing property, eventually buying small cheap houses, bringing them up to scratch and then selling at a small profit.

During this process I bought a nice semi which I could see had potential. Eagerly I started work on the first day of ownership, but the nice elderly lady neighbour who was tending her garden engaged me in conversation which was very pleasant, but after a while I got a little impatient to get on with my work programme.

Sadly, that didn't really strike her and she persisted with her stories and it became obvious she really wasn't interested in my affairs, only her own. The good lady only wanted an audience. It took me quite an embarrassing length of time to disengage, for being proud of my good manner's I let her ramble on. The next day was a recurrence, but I climbed my ladder hoping this would discourage the chatter, but Mrs Dinton followed me to the foot of the ladder and addressed me from there.

And so it went on day after day, even when I took evasive actions such as using a pneumatic drill hoping the noise would overcome her conversation, but I doubt she even noticed the din, and then by being very ill-mannered by absolutely ignoring her whilst talking to my two workmen, all to no avail.

*Around the Buoys*

Then the situation reduced to being a ridiculous comedy with her knocking on the door, causing we workmen to dash, taking evasive action by hiding under the stair's, laughing like mad in our vain effort to mislead her.

Without dragging the thing on, she really was a chatterbox and though I tried, Mrs Dinton really tested my patience until I finished the task and happily passed the house over, a very relieved man, to the Estate Agent.

Sometime later I met the neighbour who lived on the other side of the house and during our conversation I casually mentioned that Mrs Dinton could certainly tell a tale or two. "But didn't you know Bill?" she asked.

I seemed to recall hearing that question before. "Well, during the late war," she continued, "when the blitz was taking place, sadly a bomb struck her house and she had the terrible misfortune of seeing her mother being killed before her eyes. That was her mother and her home gone in a flash.

"Later, her husband was posted missing, lost at sea, and I don't think she has ever recovered from those ordeals. The results are there in her nervousness making her highly strung and terribly talkative."

Well, I thought, the poor soul has every reason to be affected with nerves like that, and maybe I should have given her a little more leeway, but she didn't seem to expect that from people like me. Possibly I should have learnt a valuable more caring lesson from Black Morgan and Teddy.

**Myself**

I don't care for drinking alcohol, never did fall in love with John Barleycorn really, it upsets my digestion, gives me a headache, and it seems to upset my comfortable way of life. I just don't think I was intended to take the stuff.

However, at the time of these events, I must admit occasionally on some late evenings, one or two whisky and water night caps gave me a pleasant glow. But if I was on my own, left to my own thoughts, at first, things seem lovely and rosy, but then I started to get a bit maudlin and introspective examining the negatives I've made of living my life.

I'm inclined to bring into the open and put under the microscope some of my faults and weaknesses, and then compare them with the shortcomings of folk I've encountered in my chequered past.

Out I drag these faults complaining and reluctant to be exposed, for normally I wouldn't admit to them being mine, however, there they stand ashamed and blushing with embarrassment, faults such as sarcasm, ingratitude, being self-opinionated, selfishness, and these just a few to start with, but I'm sure they'll more than do as an example. I then compared them with the weaknesses of past friends and workmates, deriving a little comfort and smugness when I identify some of their similar failings, things don't seem so bad then.

One evening, well into my second whisky and water, I got to thinking about Black Morgan, Teddy, and Mrs Dinton. I remembered the Bosun's crackpot idiosyncrasies and his emotional mood swings. Also, I thought of poor Teddy and his dreadful appearance and his reticent withdrawn manner, and lastly about the sad Mrs Dinton with her nervousness and uncontrollable chattering.

Sadly, I recognised the fact that all three had genuine reasons outside of their control that had caused their shortcomings, both physical and emotional. But what suddenly struck and hurt me was the realisation that I couldn't for the life of me think of any covering reasons for my own personal faults and weaknesses. There were none of those, "But didn't you know about Bill?" excuses and reasons that my friends could blame my faults on.

Still, let's say I finally learnt a lesson from the three characters I found it so easy to poke fun at.

'Oh! By the way, do your friends know of any reasons or excuses to blame your faults on?'

**His Last Voyage**

Have you ever viewed the Mersey after many months at sea?

Have you really scanned the Waterfront relieved at what you see?

Have you gazed at out stretched wings on those birds atop their perch?

Assured their moorings still secure abreast that Pied Head church?

Well, his vessels back from worldwide sights that leaves him hard to please

Yet this river holds a sense of home he's longed for overseas.

Have you ever wished the Mersey through your mind when dangers reach

Or when the Sun beats on your brow on some distant lagoon beach?

Blue gold exotic places breathe a magic to entrance

But this old seaman's eyes are quite beyond a passing glance.

His wanderlust has slowly slaked with a lifetime's kicking wheel

And his blood race only quickens when this rivers 'neath his keel

Pacific Isles and Chesapeake, the China Seas, and why so

Get excited when he's seen Port Said and Valparaiso?

*Around the Buoys*

So many years on seven seas have dulled his sense of awe

Except our salt stained waterway that floods the Seaforth shore.

He's fetched the Mersey one last time, his anchors firmly down.

His discharge book is stowed away, his pay-offs on the town.

Have you ever viewed the Mersey from the dunes at 'Sunset Strip'

You should see it through that seaman's eyes after making is last trip

When graced a lovely summers day and the Sun declines to Wales

He'll be dreaming of Tahiti or those dhows with lateen sails

With many Sunsets in his eyes, this thought may take his whim

It just could be the Sun is also setting over him.

Last port of call, he's 'Crossed the Bar' but he'll come back as he said

To squawk and swoop and join the gulls that grace our old Pier Head

So wonder at our seagulls there, their beauty begs no fault

*Bill Backshall*

And chances are you just might be admiring that 'old salt'

A saddened eye, a mournful cry, reflects his final trip

His era's dead, no more the tide will herald his tramp ship.

**Congratulations! You've managed to reach**

        **The... E**
              **N**
                **D**

Acknowledgments for Encouragement

To Gordon Tumber, for all his help with editing and presenting

For my Family, Friends, Brian Jacques and J. P. Rice-McNeill

And thanks to Hannah and all at Spinetinglers Publishing who made a dream a reality